KIDS EXPLORE
BOSTON

The very best kids' activities within an easy drive of Boston

SUSAN D. MOFFAT

BOB ADAMS, INC.
Holbrook, Massachusetts

Published by Bob Adams, Inc.
260 Center Street, Holbrook, MA 02343

ISBN: 1-55850-392-7

Printed in Korea through Sung In Printing America, Boston

A   B   C   D   E   F   G   H   I   J

Library of Congress Cataloging-in-Publication Data
Moffat, Susan D.
Kids explore Boston : the very best kids' activities within an easy drive of Boston /
Susan D. Moffat.
p.   cm.
Includes index.
ISBN: 1-55850-392-7
1. Boston Region (Mass.)—Guidebooks. 2. Children—Travel—Massachusetts—
Boston Region—Guidebooks. I. Title.
F73.18.M64   1994
917.44'610443—dc20   94-15479
                                                            CIP

This publication is designed to provide accurate and authoritative information with regard to the
subject matter covered. It is sold with the understanding that the publisher is not engaged in
rendering legal, accounting, or other professional advice. If legal advice or other expert assistance is
required, the services of a qualified professional person should be sought.
            — From a *Declaration of Principles* jointly adopted by a Committee of the
            American Bar Association and a Committee of Publishers and Associations.

Cover Design: Peter Gouck
Front Cover and Interior Photos: Susan D. Moffat (except where noted)
Rear Cover Photo: Laf Reid

This book is available at quantity discounts for bulk purchases.
For information, call 1-800-872-5627.

To Martha and Wiks, my sister and brother

TABLE OF CONTENTS

South of Boston

Cape Cod

Rhode Island

Other

Great Beaches

Cross-country Skiing

Down Hill Skiing

Index

Acknowledgments

My thanks go out to the many people who helped me along the way and made this book possible: the public relations department and directors from the many sites; and Peter Gouck, Rick Dey, Kate Layzer, Ted Agoos, Noelle and Michael Palmer, Liz Pannel, Jim Watkins, Joan and Michael Lamar, Dave Toropov, Tim and Dianna Flowers, Lauren Carson, Molly Bang, and Bob Lacey. Each provided support during the Boston adventure.

INTRODUCTION

I wrote *Kids Explore Boston* in order to help people find comprehensive, accurate information about fun places to take children within an easy drive of Boston. Although it's officially a guide for kid's activities, adults will enjoy a majority of the sites. From playgrounds to historical sites, from zoos to museums, the Boston area is loaded with exciting places for kids to play in and explore.

The mention of museums and historical sites used to bring on sighs of boredom from kids and even adults, but times have changed. Museums are no longer geared toward the adults-only crowd. "Hands-on" and "interactive" activities are featured everywhere. Since Boston holds the reputation of being a center of education, its museums emphasize and create environments for learning. Whether of science, art, computers, or history, the city's museums encourage learning through exploration.

You may feel the need to "jam it all into one visit" in order to achieve maximum satisfaction. Don't! Instead, I suggest looking over the free descriptive brochures available at most major sites and selecting exhibits or displays that most interest you. Take your time to absorb them. Enjoy.

A word of warning: Although I was careful to be very accurate about admission prices and hours, they tend to change. You might want to call ahead to confirm them.

Putting this book together has been a true adventure. I hope that you and your kids enjoy exploring Boston as much as I did.

Happy exploring!

Susan D. Moffat

FUN SCALE

🎈 **One Balloon**— Not worth any extra energy to get there, but if you do happen to be in the neighborhood, you might take a gander. The only site that gets this rating is Plymouth Rock.

🎈🎈 **Two Balloons**— Not the most fun place on the planet for kids, but it has some redeeming qualities.

🎈🎈🎈 **Three Balloons**— A middle-of-the-road on the fun scale, but worth a visit.

🎈🎈🎈🎈 **Four Balloons**— Great place, and well worth a visit.

🎈🎈🎈🎈🎈 **Five Balloons**— Wow! The ultimate in fun and definitely not to be missed.

ICON EXPLANATION

Wheelchair Accessible

Restaurant

Snackbar

Picnicking

Rest Rooms

Gift Shop

"BEST OF" RATINGS

Best of for any age
New England Aquarium, Boston
The Mapparium, Christian Science Center, Boston

Ages 2 to 4
Rhode Island Children's Museum, Pawtucket, RI
Cambridge Common Playground, Cambridge
Goodale Orchard, Ipswich

Ages 5 to 7
Rhode Island Whale and Fishing Museum, Newport, RI
Discovery Museums, Acton

Ages 8 to 10
Franklin Park Zoo, Boston
New Bedford Whaling Museum

10 and up
MIT Museum, Cambridge
The Museum of Science, Boston

BEACH NORTH OF BOSTON
Good Harbor Beach, Gloucester

BEACH SOUTH OF BOSTON
Duxbury Beach, Duxbury

CAPE COD BEACH
Paine's Creek Beach, Brewster

RESTAURANT
David's Restaurant, Newburyport

Mapparium
Christian Science Center
175 Huntington Avenue, Boston, MA 02115
(617) 450-3790

FUN SCALE

If you're used to getting stuck with parking tickets and forced to pay those exorbitant parking lot prices, you'll find it's a big relief to park in the Christian Science Center parking garage. It's clean, it's free for visitors, and the friendly attendants are more than happy to direct you to the Mapparium—which is also free and a truly remarkable place to take kids.

The Mapparium is magical. Visually, it's a little like stepping inside a colored marble; acoustically, it's the rough equivalent of an echo chamber. I'm talking about a huge globe (thirty feet in diameter), constructed entirely of stained glass panels, that visitors enter and view from the inside. When you hear echoing crystal-clear voices and find yourself surrounded by the colored panels, you'll feel like you've made it to the center of the Earth . . . and you'll be reminded again that we are all neighbors on this fragile planet.

The exhibit was constructed between 1932 and 1935, which means

that a lot of the countries shown no longer exist or are now called something else. The effect is a little unsettling: What will the world look like even two or three years from now? The people at the Mapparium have wisely avoided trying to update the exhibit, which is probably just as well. The physical structures of the earth are still essentially the same as they were in 1935, and so are the typical reactions from visitors to this Boston landmark: wonder and awe.

Take a walk around the immaculately clean complex. You'll see some remarkable architecture, including a striking fountain, known as a brick beach, and the Reflecting Pool, which manages to look perfectly flat as it spills a foot or two onto to the ground. Feel free to splash in the fountain, but stay out of the Reflecting Pool; paddling s strictly prohibited, and they mean it.

Age Range: All ages. Even the youngest will appreciate the colors and sounds of the Mapparium.
Hours: Tuesday through Friday from 9:30 a.m. to 4:00 p.m. Closed Saturday, Sunday, Monday, and some major holidays.
Admission: Free.
Time Allowance: 30 minutes.
Directions: Via the "T," take the Green Line to Hynes Auditorium. Turn left on Massachusetts Avenue. It's about three blocks down.
Parking: Free.
Wheelchair Accessible: Yes.
Restaurant: No.
Picnicking: Yes, near the fountains.
Rest Rooms: Yes.
Gift Shop: Yes, full of Christian Science-related materials.

MUSEUM OF FINE ARTS, BOSTON
465 Huntington Avenue
Boston, MA 02115
(617) 267-9300

FUN SCALE

Stretch your art appreciation to its fullest with a visit to The Museum of Fine Arts, Boston. It's an elegant and impressive space filled with captivating masterpieces from around the world from Europe and Africa to Asia and the Americas; from the early civilizations of ancient Egypt, Greece, and Rome to the art of today.

Plan ahead. To try and see the whole museum in one visit would be crazy. Kids always get a kick out of the Egyptian Gallery with its hieroglyphics, altars, and real—yes, real— mummies. Elsewhere you can admire the art of ancient Africa, located in the Nubian Gallery, the peaceful art of Asia in the Asian Art Gallery, and the shimmering art of 1870s Europe in the Impressionist collection. And don't overlook the Musical Instrument collection, or the extensive Contemporary Art collection or... the list goes on.

In addition to these permanent galleries, the rotating exhibits change regularly. Call ahead to find what's showing.

Special Childrens' Programs:

Children's Room—A *free* drop-in workshop for kids ages six through twelve. The theme changes monthly. The project changes weekly, and the one-and-a-half-hour session is broken into a group inspirational discussion based on the "art of the day," followed by a hands-on creative activity. Tuesday through Friday from 3:30 to 4:45 p.m.

Family Place—This activity happens on the first Sunday of each month from 11:00 a.m. t

4:00 p.m. The cost for the whole family is $5.00, plus museum admission. Activities are decided upon by the family and relate to specific periods and cultures of art, which change each month.

Artful Adventures—An hour-and-a-half group program for kids, ages five through eighteen, presented Tuesday through Thursday at a cost of

$45.00 per group. The program uses a hands-on approach to examine the art and social issues of different cultures. Spanish-speaking guides and teacher's guides are available.

Self-guiding booklets for families to actively explore the exhibits, including American and European paintings, Chinese, Japanese, Egyptian, and Sudanese art, are free at the Information Center and available for all levels.

Age Range: Children 2-4 no; 5 and up yes, with the right parents as guides.
Hours: Tuesday from 10:00 a.m. to 4:45 p.m., Wednesday from 10:00 a.m. to 9:45 p.m., Thursday through Sunday from 10:00 a.m. to 4:45 p.m.
West Wing special exhibitions, Thursday and Friday evenings until 9:45 p.m.
Japanese Garden, from Tuesday through Sunday 10:00 a.m. to 4:00 p.m. Closed Monday.

Admission: Adults $7.00, seniors and students $6.00, children (6-17) $3.50. Thursday and Friday evenings reduced by $1.00 for West Wing Gallery. Wednesday from 4:00 to 9:45 p.m. free.
Time Allowance: 1 1/2 to 4 hours.
Directions: Via "T," take the Green Line to the Museum stop. Cross the street and you're there.
Parking: Meter and pay-lot.
Wheelchair Accessible: Yes.
Restaurant: Cafeteria, Galleria Cafe, and Fine Arts Restaurant.
Picnicking: Yes, outside in the courtyard or in the Cafeteria downstairs.
Rest Rooms: Yes.
Gift Shop: Yes; open Tuesday and Saturday from 10:00 a.m. to 4:30 p.m.; Wednesday through Friday from 10:00 a.m. to 9:30 p.m.; Sunday noon to 4:30 p.m. Full of exciting books, prints, jewelry, and games.

BOSTON PUBLIC LIBRARY
666 Boylston Street
Boston, MA 02117
(617) 536-5400

FUN SCALE

The Boston Public Library (BPL) is the oldest free municipal library in the United States. Forget the books; even a promenade through this extraordinary century-old edifice is worth your time. Climb the worn marble staircase to the third-floor Wiggin Gallery and view one of the art exhibits (they change regularly). Wander into the Italian villa-styled courtyard and surround yourself with the splendor of lush plants and bubbling fountains. (Oh, well; maybe it wouldn't hurt to take along a good book!)

Needless to say, the BPL's resources are extensive. Borrowing privileges are free to all state residents: Show a picture ID and seconds later you'll receive an official BPL card (assuming you're not already on the "wanted" list for overdue books, that is.)

The Children's Room is designed to nurture a love of reading, listening, and learning. There are shelves and shelves of books, as well as friendly staff people close by to help. There are many scheduled kids' events, too; call for information.

Age Range: Any age. Even the youngest child loves to be read to.
Hours: Monday through Thursday from 9:00 a.m. to 9:00 p.m. Friday and Saturday from 9:00 a.m. to 5:00 p.m. Closed Sunday.
Admission: Free.
Directions: Via the "T," take the Green Line to Copley Square.
Parking: Meter and pay-lot.
Wheelchair Accessible: Yes.
Restaurant: No, but within an easy walk.
Picnicking: No, but walk over to Copley Square and picnic away.
Rest Rooms: Yes.
Gift Shop: No.

CLARENDON STREET PLAYGROUND
Clarendon Street
Boston
(617) 247-3961 (committee number)

FUN SCALE

If you're looking for a well-kept, safe, seemingly private but open-to-the-public playground, look no further than the Clarendon Street Playground. There are swings, slides, a jungle gym, and wooden climbing structures. Scattered about are toys left by forgetful children. You can be pretty sure the toys will be there when the kids return. The playground's atmosphere is one of care and honesty.

Climb aboard the wooden block car and pretend you're driving down the traffic-free streets of Boston (dream on!). Later, enjoy a picnic under the shade of one of the willow trees.

Several annual events are sponsored by the Clarendon Street Committee, ranging from Easter Egg Hunts to Halloween festivities. Call for information.

Hours: 8:00 a.m. to 6:00 p.m..
Directions: Via the "T," take the Green Line to Copley Square Station.
Parking: Meter and pay-lot.
Wheelchair Accessible: Yes.
Picnicking: Yes.
Rest Rooms: No.

15

MUSEUM OF AFRO-AMERICAN HISTORY
African Meeting House
46 Joy Street, Boston, MA 02114
(617) 742-1854

FUN SCALE

The Afro-American History Museum, which could be combined with the Black Heritage Trail Tour (see below), is worth a visit. The goal of the museum is to educate people through the changing exhibits about the rich historical legacy of Afro-Americans in the New England area.

The African Meeting House, which is next door, is the oldest black church still standing in the USA. Created in 1806, it's loaded with architectural and cultural history. It was a major religious, educational, social, and political center for Boston's black community in the nineteenth century.

Today the pleasantly lighted and simple structure houses various programs, lectures, and musical events. There's a changing gallery space that exhibits African art addressing issues of Afro-America from the eighteenth to the twentieth century. There is also a summer camp program for kids aged from nine to fifteen years that includes workshops on drumming, mask making, Caribbean culture, and public speaking.

Age Range: Kids 2-4 no; 5-7 possibly, with guidance; 8 and up yes, with guidance.
Hours: Monday through Friday 10:00 a.m. to 4:00 p.m.
Admission: Free.
Time Allowance: 30 to 60 minutes.
Directions: Via the "T," take the Red Line to Park Street Station. Walk up to Beacon Street and turn left. Take a right on Joy Street and it's up the hill on the left.
Parking: Meter (good luck) and pay-lot.
Wheelchair Accessible: No.
Restaurant: No.
Picnicking: No.
Rest Rooms: Yes.
Gift Shop: Yes; books, prints, T-shirts.

BLACK HERITAGE TRAIL TOUR
African Meeting House
46 Joy Street, Boston, MA 02114
(617) 742-1854

FUN SCALE

The Black Heritage Trail is a 1.6-mile walking tour that explores the history of Boston's Afro-American community. Pick a nice day, have a cup of coffee or Gatorade, put on your walking shoes, and go to Shaw Memorial, where the tour begins. Follow the tour from site to site (there are fourteen) through the largest concentration of pre-Civil War Afro-American historic sites in the USA. The walk ends at the **African Meeting House**, the oldest black church still standing.

It's a two-hour stroll through history. The tour can be joined at any of the fifteen sites, or self-guide booklets can be obtained at the **Afro-American History Museum**. The tour might not be so much fun for young children, but it's worthwhile for those old enough to understand the importance of Afro-American history.

Age: Kids 2-7—it's a hike, and might be too much for little legs; 8 and up yes, but not necessarily for the whole tour.
Hours: From Memorial Day to Labor Day, 10:00 a.m., 12:00 noon, 2:00 p.m.
Admission: Free.
Time Allowance: 2 hours.
Directions: Via the "T," take the Red Line to Park Street Station. Walk up to Beacon Street and turn left. Take a right on Joy Street and it's up the hill on the left. The tour begins at Shaw Memorial on Beacon Street.
Parking: Meter.

THE SWAN BOATS
Boston, Public Garden
(617) 522-1966

FUN SCALE

A definite "don't miss" in Boston in the warmer months are the Swan Boats located in the Public Garden across the street from Boston Common. The boats look exactly like the drawings in Robert McClosky's 1941 children's classic, *Make Way for Ducklings*.

Embark on one of these vessels and you'll experience fifteen minutes of splendor in a boat that's foot-propelled by large-muscled, human peddlers enclosed by a large swan-like construction. The boats skim gracefully through the lagoon's waters surrounded by trees, grass, and fleets of swimming ducks for a truly pastoral effect. Some people like to bring a snack for the ducks. It's a nice break from the hustle and bustle of city life.

The idea, conceived and executed by Robert Paget in 1877, was based on the opera *Lohengrin*, in which a princess is rescued by a knight in a boat pulled by a swan. To this day the swan boat business is run by later generations of the Paget family.

For hard-core realists, this fairy tale thing may be a bit far-fetched. But for kids, what better way to spend part of a day in Boston than to be pulled along in a boat by a giant swan? The experience is a magical one for the price.

And by the way, don't forget to visit the bronze sculptures of Mrs. Mallard and her eight ducklings, Jack, Kack, Lack, Mack, Nack, Ouack, Pack, and Quack, the legendary family of Robert McClosky's timeless story. The ducks are large enough to climb on—and are a perfect photo opportunity—so bring your camera!

Age Range: All ages.

Hours: Patriot's Day to June 20, daily from 10:00 a.m. to 4:00 p.m.; June 21 through Labor Day daily from 10:00 a.m. to 5:00 p.m.; Labor Day to September 19 weekdays from noon to 4:00 p.m.; weekends from 10:00 a.m. to 4:00 p.m.

Admission: Adults $1.50, children (under 12) 95¢.

Time allowance: 15 minutes.

Directions: Via the "T," take the Red Line to the Park Street Station.

Parking: Meter and Charles Street Garage.

Wheelchair Accessible: Yes.

Restaurant: No, but within walking distance.

Picnicking: Yes.

Rest rooms: No.

Gift Shop: Yes; postcards, T-shirts, tote bags.

BOSTON COMMON PLAYGROUND
Surrounded by Beacon, Charles, Boylston, Park, and Tremont Streets.

FUN SCALE

Boston Common has been around since 1634. The country's oldest park, it's loaded with history. Your kids may be interested to know, for instance, that the Common originated as a "common ground" for cows and other grazing animals. Today it's the center of much excitement, with strollers, joggers, musical events, and demonstrations—and it's a great playground for kids.

In the playground, you and the kids will want to climb the rope ladders, slide down the slide, crawl through a tunnel, and do all of the things people do in playgrounds. Then, in the summer, you can hop on over to the Frog Pond for a little respite from the heat. It's a gigantic, shallow wading pool with a spraying fountain for kids to splash around in.

Numerous kids' events take place on the Common throughout the year. Some are one-time happenings; others are repeated year after year.

June's **Dairy Festival** is a money raiser for the Dana Farber Cancer Institute. For $3.00 it's an "all you can eat" ice cream fest, where you can lick your cones in the company of local bovines and farmers. Holy cow!

Another annual summer event is sponsored by **Oxfam America**. The peace-promoting festival features African art, music, and food. A fun event and a worthwhile cause.

August holds the **Festival of Hope** celebration. This valuable and charitable event makes use of school programs to promote peace. It's all done to the tune of live music, food and demonstrations.

The **Teddy Bear Picnic**, another June event, is free and a lot of fun for teddy bear fans. Bring your teddy for a night on the town. Experience the Rosenshontz Folk Duo and check out all the other teddies. The picnic lasts from 6-8 p.m. during the month of June. Bring your own picnic.

The park is legally open for passage twenty-four hours a day. For obvious reasons of safety, however, the suggested hours are from dawn to dusk.

Hours: Dawn to dusk.
Admission: Free.
Directions: Via the "T," take the Red Line to Park Street Station.
Parking: Meter (watch your time).
Wheelchair Accessible: Yes.
Restaurant: Not in the park, but close by.
Picnicking: Yes.
Rest Rooms: No.

THE SKYWALK
Prudential Tower
Boylston Street, Boston, MA 02116
(617) 236-3318

FUN SCALE

For an ear-popping rush, take the thirty-two-second express elevator ride to the fiftieth floor of the Prudential Tower. Yawn a few times to clear your ears and step out to an incredible panoramic view of Boston. Out of the western windows you can see the famous Fenway Park and the stately headquarters of The First Church of Christ Scientist; to the north, the New Hampshire mountains, the Museum of Science, and the MIT campus. Look east and you'll see Trinity Church, Boston Harbor, and the rival tower of the John Hancock Building. (The John Hancock Observatory is sixty stories high; the Prudential Tower, although shorter, has antennae that, so it claims, make it slightly taller. So there.) On a clear day, looking southward, you may be able to catch a glimpse of Cape Cod.

Age Range: Any age, if not afraid of heights.
Hours: Monday through Saturday from 10:00 a.m. to 10:00 p.m., Sunday from 12:00 noon to 10:00 p.m.
Admission: Adults $2.75; seniors, students with college ID, and children (5-15) $1.75.
Time Allowance: 30 to 60 minutes.
Directions: Via the "T," take the Green Line to the Prudential stop and head for the Prudential Tower.
Parking: Parking garage in building or meter.
Wheelchair Accessible: Yes.
Restaurant: No, but nearby.
Picnicking: No.
Rest Rooms: Yes.
Gift Shop: Yes; T-shirts, post cards.

JOHN HANCOCK OBSERVATORY
John Hancock Tower
Copley Square, Boston, MA 02116
(617) 247-1977

FUN SCALE

Towering over the heart of Boston, the John Hancock Observatory is the tallest building in all of New England. Board the express elevator and fly to the sixtieth floor in a matter of seconds. Disembark and look around. A bird's-eye view of all of Boston lies below you. From every window history and excitement prevail. Circle around and see such sights as the historic South End, the site of the Boston Tea Party, the Bunker Hill Monument, Fenway Park, the JFK Library, and even the pub that inspired TV's *Cheers*! Fact-filled informational audio-visual panels accompany you around the Observatory. Skyline Boston provides you with a narration of the dramatic changes that transformed Boston from a small peninsula town to the booming city before you. For a closer view, a quarter will buy you a look through a high-powered telescope focused on some of Boston's major attractions.

Age Range: Any age, if not afraid of heights.
Hours: Monday through Saturday from 9:00 a.m. to 11:00 p.m., Sunday from 10:00 a.m. to 11:00 p.m. (May through October); 12:00 noon to 11:00 p.m. (November through April).
Admission: Adults $3.00, seniors and children (5-17) $2.25.
Time Allowance: About 1 hour.
Directions: Via the "T," take the Green Line to Copley Square or the Orange Line to Back Bay Station.
Parking: Meter or parking garage behind Observatory.
Wheelchair Accessible: Yes.
Restaurant: No, but nearby.
Picnicking: No.
Rest Rooms: Yes.
Gift Shop: Yes; postcards, magazines, T-shirts.

NEWBURY COMICS
332 Newbury Street
Boston, MA 02115
(617) 236-4930

FUN SCALE

If you're looking for the best supply of comic books, head over to Newbury Comics. X Men, Batman, Donald Duck, Teenage Mutant Ninja Turtle comic books and all your favorites, plus numerous posters, CDs, T-shirts, and baseball caps can be found there.

Age Range: There are some comics for younger kids, but the majority are geared toward the 10-and-up range.
Directions: Via the "T," take the Green Line to Copley Square, walk one block down to Newbury Street, and turn left.
Parking: Meter and pay-lot.
Wheelchair Accessible: No.
Rest Rooms: No.

TRINITY CHURCH
Copley Square
Boston, MA 02116
(617) 536-0944

FUN SCALE

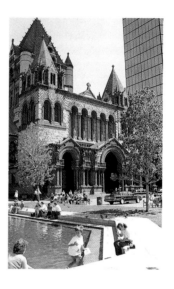

Towering above Copley Square and surrounded by other architectural greats, such as the John Hancock Tower and the Boston Public Library, Trinity Church is well worth a visit. Built between 1872 and 1877, this National Historic Landmark is considered one of the most architecturally important buildings of the nineteenth century. Even your kids will be awestruck as they gaze around the church's interior. Notice the rich conglomeration of architectural styles. Except during church services, funerals, and weddings, tours are available every thirty minutes and are free.

Age Range: Kids 2-4 no; 5-10 yes, for a quick peek at the church (the tour probably wouldn't be of interest); 10 and up, definitely good for a peek and possibly for the tour.
Hours: Daily from 8:00 a.m. to 6:00 p.m.
Admission: Free.
Time Allowance: Half an hour.
Directions: Via "T," take the Green Line to Copley Square.
Parking: Meter and pay-lot.
Wheelchair Accessible: Yes.
Restaurant: No.
Picnicking: Yes; great spots in Copley Square.
Rest Rooms: Yes.
Gift Shop: No.

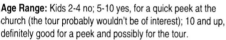

FENWAY PARK TOUR
4 Yawkay Way
Boston, MA 02215
(617) 236-6666.

FUN SCALE

Take me out to the ball game! If you're a fan of America's national sport, you won't want to miss this forty-minute tour of the home of the Boston Red Sox. Meet at Gate D for a stroll through eighty years of Red Sox history.

The tour begins on the fifth floor with behind-the-scenes views of the executive rooms, the media dining room, and the press box. Check out the style in which important people see ball games.

On the fourth floor are the private suites, available for a mere $1,400 per game; these include a TV, kitchen, and private balcony. The 600 Club is also located on the fourth floor. For a mere $8 zillion (approximately!), you can be a member for four years, a privilege that includes really comfortable seats and the right to purchase fine food and drinks from the private restaurant.

Unless the field is wet, you'll be able to go out on the field via the "warning track" and touch the infamous GREEN MONSTER, the home run wall. Feel the excitement of sitting in the dugout and looking at the field from a player's perspective. Try to stump the knowledgeable guide with one of those impossible baseball questions. The forty-minute experience is a baseball fan's dream.

Age Range: Kids 2-4 no; 5-7 possibly, if with an enthusiastic parent; 8 and up yes, if baseball fan.
Hours: Early May until late September, Monday through Friday at 10:00 a.m., 11:00 a.m., 12:00 noon, and 1:00 p.m.
Admission: Adults $5.00, seniors $4.00, kids (15 and under) $2.50. Advance reservation recommended.
Time Allowance: 40 minutes.
Directions: Via the "T," take the Green Line to Fenway Station.
Parking: Meter or pay-lot.
Wheelchair Accessible: Yes.
Restaurant: Not inside the Park, but plenty within walking distance.
Picnicking: No.
Rest Rooms: Yes.
Gift Shop: No, but many surround the Park.

CHARLES RIVER PLAYGROUNDS
Around the Hatch Shell
Storrow Drive
Boston

FUN SCALE

There are two semi-nameless playgrounds sandwiched between the busy Charles River and the even busier Storrow Drive; the location alone makes them exciting play spaces. For lack of any other names, I'll call the one east of the Hatch Shell the Esplanade Playground and the one west of the Hatch Shell the Fiedler Playground. The Esplanade Playground, designed for toddlers, features swings in the shape of ducks, turtles, and other goofy creatures. It is fenced in. The Fieldler Playground, on the other side of the Hatch Shell and across the footbridge, is also fenced; it provides bigger-kid equipment such as climbing structures. Make sure you take note of the wacky statue of Arthur Fieldler (a former Conductor of The Boston Pops) along the way, and look for ducks in the Canoe Way as you cross the footbridge.

Directions: Via the "T," take the Red Line to Charles Street Circle or the Green Line to Arlington Street.
Parking: Meter and pay-lot across Storrow Drive. Use a nearby footbridge to cross.
Restaurant: Snack bar.
Picnicking: Yes.
Rest Rooms: Yes.

27

BOSTON COMMUNITY BOATING
JUNIOR PROGRAM
21 Embankment Road, Boston, MA 02114
(617) 523-1038

FUN SCALE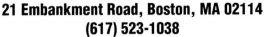

If you're between ten and seventeen years old, can swim seventy-five yards, and come with a parental permission slip, you can learn all about rowing and sailing in the Boston Community Boating Program. It only costs $1.00 per season for lessons and use of the equipment. Learn how to operate a thirteen-foot single-sailed Laser or a Mistral wind surfer, to name a few, under the instruction of expert kid sailors. If you get good enough, join the Junior Racing Team. There are many organized events in which to partake. In addition to sailing, the blueberry-pie-eating contest is a favorite.

Age Range: 10-17 years.
Hours: Labor Day through late August, Monday to Friday from 9:00 a.m. to 3:00 p.m.
Admission: $1.00 per season.
Directions: Via the "T," take the Red Line to Charles Street and cross over the footbridge to the Charles River boat basin.
Parking: Meter and pay-lot across Storrow Drive.
Wheelchair Accessible: No.
Restaurant: Snack bar.
Picnicking: Yes.
Rest Rooms: Yes.

THE HATCH SHELL
Storrow Drive
Boston, MA 02114
(617) 727-5215

FUN SCALE

The Hatch Shell, constructed in the shape of a half shell, is the site of numerous performances and entertaining events. The shows range from Friday flicks to all sorts of musical events and are billed as family entertainment. So take your blanket or mat and head over to the Hatch Shell for some free entertainment alongside the Charles River.

Hours: Vary with show.
Admission: Free.
Directions: Via the "T," take the Red Line to Charles Street Circle or the Green Line to Arlington Street.
Parking: Limited parking is allowed on Storrow Drive during the performances. Otherwise, meter and pay-lot across Storrow Drive. Use a footbridge to cross.
Wheelchair Accessible: Yes.
Restaurant: Snack bar.
Picnicking: Yes.
Rest Rooms: Yes.

NEW ENGLAND AQUARIUM
Central Wharf
Boston, MA 02110-3399
(617) 973-5200

FUN SCALE

With vivid banners flying overhead and a Susumu Shingu sculpture dancing in the wind, the New England Aquarium, perched at the edge of Boston harbor, is easy to spot. In an outdoor tank near the entrance, harbor seals frolic almost close enough to touch.

The inside scene is even more colorful and active. The centerpiece of the aquarium, a massive 187,000-gallon ocean tank, is one of the world's largest cylindrical salt-water tanks. It's filled with tropical fish, humongous sea turtles, ferocious-looking sharks, and realistic features of artificial rock and coral, with tunnels and caves for slippery eels to dart around in. Interestingly enough, all sea life swims counter clockwise and against the water current. A broad ramp spirals around the outside of the tank, affording visitors of all ages an unobstructed view of the creatures inside, even on crowded days. Ascend the stairs at the top of the ramp and you're at the edge looking down inside the amazing structure. A shark's fin cuts the surface. Wow! Feeding is done by scuba divers five times a day.

At the tank's periphery are other exotic exhibits. Some change on a regular basis; others are on permanent display. The penguins are a perennial favorite. Did yo know that not all penguins live in cold climates? The aquarium's Rockhopper and

Blackfooted penguins are warm-weather species and are perfectly content to swir and play in their pool at the base of the ocean tank. Watch them hop around on rocks and skim through the water. Fun!

Moving along to the "Edge of the Sea" exhibit, g ready to touch something cold and wet and slimy— or prickly, or rough, or soft... C course, you might get slight wet in the process. A

sensory adventure! The tide pool exhibit features a realistic simulation of New England's shoreline for kids to climb on. Pick up a starfish or play with a harmless horseshoe crab, while a friendly staff member answers your questions.

Don't miss the sea lion presentations, which take place five times a day on board the *Discovery*. This unusual floating pavilion provides a twenty-minute, conservation-oriented presentation with the goal of increasing audience awareness in a fun way. Using a variety of props, including a giant six-pack yoke and a laundry detergent bottle, the massive marine animals and their trainers demonstrate the dangers of plastic pollutants and hint at some solutions.

Other Programs:

The New England Aquarium also offers other sea programs. **Science at Sea**, an hour-and-a-half harbor cruise, is a great opportunity for kids and other budding scientists to learn and have fun. Participants can haul a lobster trap, take a plankton tow, or buttonhole one of the ship's naturalists for the answer to one of those nagging science questions, like, "Why do lobsters always have rubber bands on their claws?" It's not only so they don't snap an unsuspecting finger off, as you might assume; it's also because because they're cannibals and would otherwise eat each other. Of course, even if you don't want to try your hand at lobstering, there's nothing like a relaxing harbor cruise. Sit back and enjoy the view as the voyage takes you past the World Trade Center and Logan Airport, with the jets coming alarmingly close overhead. I'll bet you didn't know there was a population of endangered Snowy Owls in the rocks alongside the airport. Seem strange? The secret is rats. Yes, there's quite a large population of rats in that area.

You'll also cruise past Spectacle Island—appropriately nicknamed "Garbage Island" after serving as Boston's dumping

ground from the 1930s to the 1950s— and Thompson Island, one of the harbor's prettiest. The return trip will take you along the Charlestown side of the harbor and past the U.S.S. *Constitution*.

From spring until fall the Aquarium offers **whale watches**, a definite must. A 103-foot vessel takes you to Stellwagon Bank, twenty-four miles from Boston, a rich feeding ground for humpack whales, finback whales, dolphins, and other marine mammals. When the whales feel frisky, they may jump completely out of the water, which is called "breeching." Have your cameras ready! The trip lasts for approximately five hours. Food is available on board, or you may bring your own. Reservations are necessary; children must be over thirty-six inches tall. Your experience will tell you whether your child can endure a five-hour boatride.

GENERAL AQUARIUM

Age range: Any age will be sure to appreciate the experience. See age comments for Science at Sea and the Whale Watch.

Hours:

Winter Hours (Day after Labor Day through June 30) Monday through Wednesday from 9:00 a.m. to 5:00 p.m.; Thursday from 9:00 a.m. to 8:00 p.m.; Friday from 9:00 a.m. to 5:00 p.m.; Saturday, Sunday, Holidays from 9:00 a.m. to 6:00 p.m.

Closed Christmas Day, Thanksgiving Day. Open at noon on New Year's Day.

Summer Hours (July 1 through Labor Day) Monday, Tuesday, Friday from 9:00 a.m. to 6:00 p.m.; Wednesday, Thursday from 9:00 a.m. to 8:00 p.m.; Saturday, Sunday, Holidays from 9:00 a.m. to 7:00 p.m.

Admission:

General (12 years and up) $8.50, kids (3-11) $4.50, seniors $7.50.

Thursdays and summer Wednesdays from 4:00 p.m. to 7:30 p.m., $1.00 all admission prices.

Time Allowance: 1-3 hours.

Directions: Via the "T," take the Blue Line to the Aquarium Station.

Parking: Meter and pay-lot.

Wheelchair Accessible: Yes.

Restaurant: Snack bar outside.

Picnicking: Yes.

Rest Rooms: Yes, with changing tables.
Gift Shop: Yes; T-shirts, puzzles, games, cool prints.

HARBOR TOURS; SCIENCE AT SEA

Spring and Fall Hours (March to June, September to December)

Departs	Returns
9:00 a.m.	10:45 a.m.
11:15 a.m.	1:00 p.m.
1:30 p.m.	3:15 p.m.
3:30 p.m.	5:15 p.m.

Summer Schedule (July to mid-September)

Departs	Returns
10:30 a.m.	12:00 p.m.
12:30 p.m.	2:00 p.m.
2:30 p.m.	4:00 p.m.
4:30 p.m.	6:00 p.m.
7:00 p.m.*	8:30 p.m.

* Wednesday and Thursday evenings only.

Rates:	Harbor Boat	NEAq Member/ Group Rate	Combo with Aquarium
Adults	$8.50	$7.50	$12.00
Seniors	$6.50	$6.00	$12.00
Youth (12-18)	$6.50	$6.00	$10.00
Children (under 12)	$5.50	$5.25	$8.50
School Groups		$5.25	$8.50

One free chaperone per 5 youths.
Groups consist of 15 or more.

WHALE WATCH

Rates	General	NEAq Member/ Group Rate*
General Admission	$23.00	$18.50
Senior Citizens & College Students	$18.50	$17.00
Youths (12-18)	$17.00	$15.00
Children (3-11)**	$16.00	$15.00
Youth Groups (K-12)	$15.00	

1 Free Chaperone per 10 Youths
(extra chaperones— $15.00)

*Group Rates are for 15 or more.
** Children must be over 36 inches tall.
Daily trips from April through October.
Call (617)973-5277 for scheduled times.

THE CHILDREN'S MUSEUM
300 Congress St.
Boston, MA 02210
(617) 426-6500

FUN SCALE

Copyright © The Children's Museum

Words can only graze the surface of the Children's Museum. It's huge! Room after room of hands-on activities and exhibits, covering a broad range of subjects, all manage to reflect the museum's philosophy that real objects, direct experiences, and enjoyment support learning.

Take the **Kid's Bridge**, for instance. It's a lesson on connecting the barriers between populations, and it's done by exposure to fun and stimulating activities.

Kids are exposed to other cultures and countries throughout the museum. **Teen Tokyo** is based on life in contemporary Japan. Visit a Japanese home, but don't forget to take your shoes off before entering! Hop on the full-sized subway car, complete with sound effects. Pit your strength against a life-sized replica of a sumo wrestler. Sing along with the karaoke box. Design Japanese-influenced animation with the computer.

If you're into recycling, and you should be, step into the **Recycle Shop** and pick up a few art materials. For very little money you can make something new and wonderful with materials once designated for throwing away. You'll be amazed at what you find!

There are toddler activities too. The **Toddler Area**, for ages four and under (adult supervision, of course), provides a space for finger painting, story listening, and other activities. There are dress-ups, climbing structures, and a toy car to ride in. There's even a space for infants! The **Bric Block Room** is also great for little ones. You'll find giant, and I mean giant, Leggos on a carpeted floor. Your preschoolers will feel as if they're in heaven!

Migrate into the **Science Playground** and learn about things like motion and gravity through ski jumps, spirals, and motion dishes. The bubbles are always a big hit

Studio 1015 is for older kids (aged appropriately, 10 through 15). It offers them the chance to get together with others of the same age, vent concerns, and develop

...eadership and creativity. It's a happening place, and includes a Swamp Resource Room with swamp creature chairs and underwater murals, a Mess Room with a stove and fridge, and a multipurpose room where kids can dance, exercise, and attend Friday evening workshops.

Age Range: There's something for every age...even adults.

Hours: July 1 through Labor Day, daily from 10:00 a.m. to 5:00 p.m., and Fridays until 9:00 p.m. September through June, closed Mondays except Boston school vacations and holidays.

Admission: Adults $7.00, kids (2-15) and seniors $6.00, one-year-olds $2.00. Fridays from 5:00 to 9:00 p.m., $1.00 for all.

Time Allowance: 2 to 4 hours.

Directions: Via the "T," take the Red Line to South Station. Exit, walk down Congress Street, across Fort Point Channel, and to the museum.

Parking: Pay-lot.

Wheelchair Accessible: Yes.

Restaurant: Yes; McDonald's and The Milk Bottle Cafe.

Picnicking: Yes, outside.

Rest Rooms: Yes, with changing tables.

Gift Shop: Yes; from books about icky bugs to "Gooey Dino Soap" to plain old hoola hoops.

COMPUTER MUSEUM
300 Congress Street
Boston, MA 02210
(617) 423-6758

FUN SCALE

Copyright © Dan McCoy

You don't have to be computer literate to have fun with these 125 plu hands-on exhibits. The Computer Museum offers exciting and accessib experiences for all.

The **Walk-Through Computer** is a journey inside a computer fifty times larger than life. Climb on the 25 foot operational keyboard and spin the giant trackball. Inside the computer, check out the memory chips and pulsing neon lights. Wow!

Visit the interactive learning stations, software theater, and viewports. In **People and Computers Milestones of a Revolution** you'll travel through "time tunnels" tracing the computer's evolution from the room-sized behemoths of the 1940s to the present-day microprocessors and laptops. It's educational— and also a lot of fun.

Visitors as young as four years can enjoy the various interactive activities. Try drawing on the wall with a giant laser-guided wand over a wall-sized projection of a computer paint program. Be your own band by using a Musical Instrument Digital Interface (MIDI) system to add trumpet, drum, or piano tracks to one of four prerecorded compositions. Explore a strange universe with a cartoon guide named Osmo in **Comic Osmo**.

For you older kids, why not learn how a spreadsheet works by "spending" a million dollars? Or you can plan a wedding reception with a time

management program that will help you organize all the details. Check out the **Bodyworks** exhibit and use an anatomy database to explore the human body from skin to skeleton.

Even if you're scared to death of computers, you'll enjoy Boston's Computer Museum. Just don't be too shocked if your school-aged kids know more about how to use them than you do!

Age Range: 2-4 doubtful; 5 and up yes.
Hours: Summer, daily from 10:00 a.m. to 6:00 p.m.
Winter, Tuesday through Sunday from 10:00 a.m. to 5:00 p.m.
Admission: Adults $7.00, students and seniors $5.00, kids 4 and under free.
Time Allowance: 1 and 1/2 to 3 hours.
Directions: Via the "T," take the Red Line to South Station. Exit, walk toward the water, cross Fort Point Channel, and you're here.
Parking: Pay-lot.
Wheelchair Accessible: Yes.
Restaurant: MacDonald's and Milk Bottle Cafe.
Picnicking: Yes.
Restrooms: Yes.
Gift Shop: Yes; T-shirts, games, posters.

BOSTON TEA PARTY SHIP AND MUSEUM
Congress Street Bridge
Boston, MA 02210
(617) 338-1773

FUN SCALE

Copyright © Boston Tea Party Museum

Boston has long been famous for the big Tea Party of December 16, 1773. As an act of defiance toward the British Parliament for the unpopular tea tax, a group of American colonists boarded three British tea ships and dumped hundreds of chests of tea into the harbor.

Reenact the event through the museum's audiovisuals and by climbing aboard the *Beaver II*, a brigantine and a working replica of one of the three original Tea Party ships. Explore the quarters below decks. Claustrophobics beware, it's cramped down here! Check out the 10,200 feet of rigging and experience the hands-on knot-tying board. Finally, throw a crate of tea into the harbor and retrieve it by hauling on a block and tackle. Questions can be answered by the costumed and animated guides.

The Tea Party Ship and Museum are conveniently located next to the Children's and Computer Museums.

Age Range: 2-4 doubtful; 5-7 possibly; 8 and up yes. (A basic knowledge of American history is helpful.)
Hours: Spring and fall, daily from 9:00 a.m. to 5:00 p.m.
Summer, daily from 9:00 a.m. to 6:00 p.m.
Closed Thanksgiving, Christmas, and New Year's Day.
Admission: Adults $6.00, kids (5-14) $3.00.
Time Allowance: 45 minutes or less.
Directions: Via the "T," take the Red Line to South Station. Exit and walk to Fort Point Channel.
Parking: Meter and pay-lot.
Wheelchair Accessible: No.
Restaurant: Not at the museum, but next door is MacDonald's and the Milk Bottle Cafe.
Picnicking: Yes, with prearranged permission.
Rest Rooms: Yes.
Gift shop: Yes; T-shirts, tea pots, teas, and Indian feathers.

CHRISTOPHER COLUMBUS WATERFRONT PARK
Commercial Wharf, Boston

FUN SCALE

Kids can climb, slide, or make believe on wooden playground equipment reminiscent of ships at sea, all against a background of Boston harbor. With such a nautical environment it's not difficult to imagine boarding one of the many ships in the harbor, sailing out to sea, fighting off pirates, catching a colossal octopus, navigating to new lands, and returning for a giant ice-cream cone on shore!

It's a fantastic space to have a picnic lunch, throw a Frisbee, or relax on a park bench under the shade provided by the trellises. There are plenty of benches and ledges, along with vendors selling caps, cards, and ice cream. If you want something more substantial in the way of a meal, outdoor restaurants border the park.

Directions: Via the "T," take the Blue Line to the Aquarium Station. Turn right on Atlantic Ave and it's one block down.
Parking: Meter and pay-lot.
Wheelchair Accessible: Yes.
Picnicking: Yes.
Rest Rooms: No.

QUINCY MARKETPLACE
Congress Street
Boston, MA 02109
(617) 338-2323

FUN SCALE

This classic stop on the tourist trail is a cornucopia of shops and eateries. The long, two-floored building houses food stand upon food stand, and shop upon shop, all fun stuff. The surrounding buildings are also full of shopping options. Choose among the Disney Store, Kid's Unlimited, Raggedy Alley Gallery, The City Zoo, Boston Brownie, and Aris Barbecue. . . to name only a few.

Hours: Monday through Saturday from 10:00 a.m. to 9:00 p.m., Sunday from 12:00 noon to 6:00 p.m.
Admission: Free.
Directions: Via the "T," take the Green Line to Government Center, cross the plaza, go down the steps, cross the street, and you're there.
Parking: Meter, pay-lot, or garage.
Wheelchair Accessible: Yes.
Restaurant: Yes, many.
Picnicking: Yes.
Rest Rooms: Yes.

MUSEUM OF SCIENCE
Science Park
Boston, MA 02114
(617) 723-2500

FUN SCALE

Plan to spend a full day at The Museum of Science. In this vast collection of exhibits, some permanent and some "special," you'll experience science in its most mind-blowing and exciting forms. It's a heavily hands-on, interactive approach to learning, with hundreds of fun-filled things to see and do related to just about every branch of the sciences.

The **Theater of Electricity**, for instance, one of the permanent exhibits, features live demos of lightening, static electricity, corona, and other phenomena.

The **Human Body Discovery Space** allows you to test your senses of smell and taste, look through a microscope at grains of pepper (they look like rocks), and test your ability to lie on a monitor that measures how much electricity the skin is conducting through temperature changes.

Check out the humongous wave tank in the **Fluidica Hall** or the life-sized model **Tyrannosaurus Rex** on the basement level. Its face gazes through the Plexiglas barrier on the first floor! For something closer to home, experience **The Big Dig**, which will give you the scoop on Boston's Central Artery/Tunnel Project. Enter the simulated elevator ride down to the "harbor floor," where you'll look at various worksites through eye holes in a fence and see a 3-D video of the workers in action. This particular exhibit will be up until the excavation has been completed—in ten or twenty years!

For a truly cosmic experience, visit the **Charles Hayden Planetarium** for a fascinating look at astronomical images and discoveries.

The Mugar Omni Theater features a state-of-the-art film projection and sound system for a very *real* view of whatever is showing at the time. You're surrounded by a domed screen wrapping over and around you, and blasting out sounds through eighty-four loudspeakers. Talk about a 3-D experience!

If you need a food break, go to the Museum Cafe on the first floor, Friendly's Restaurant on the second floor, or The Skyline Restaurant on the sixth floor. The Museum Shop has some cool things to take home.

Age Range: Kids 2-4 will benefit from some of the interactive activities, but the Omni Theater may be a bit much. For ages 5 and up, there's something for almost everyone at the museum.

Hours: Daily from 9:00 a.m. to 5:00 p.m., Friday from 9:00 a.m. to 9:00 p.m.

Admission: Museum Exhibits— Adults $7.00, children and seniors $5.00. Omni Theater—Adults $7.00, children and seniors $5.00. Planetarium show—Adults $6.00, children and seniors $4.00. Combo ticket discounts are available.

Time Allowance: A minimum of two hours; more if you decide to go to any theater shows. The museum is always good for repeat visits.

Directions: Via the "T," take the Green Line to Science Park and follow the signs.

Parking: At the museum garage there's plenty of parking for a fee.

Wheelchair Accessible: Yes.

Restaurant: Museum Cafe, Friendly's, and The Skyline Restaurant.

Picnicking: No.

Rest Rooms: Yes.

Gift Shop: Yes; jewelry, books, magic rocks, T-shirts, models.

HAYES PARK
Corner of West Canton and Warren Avenues
Boston

FUN SCALE

The Hayes Park (its official name) sits gracefully amid the gentrified brownstones of Boston. A new play space, it is not known by any particular name among those who frequent it, but is highly thought of as a quiet haven. A statue of a child by Kahlil Gibran (no, not the renowned writer, but his great-nephew, who lives down the block) acts as the centerpiece. Well-kept, cheery gardens encircle the park. The minimalist playground equipment fits the mood of quiet play.

Hours: From dawn to 11:30 p.m.
Directions: Via the "T," take the Green Line to Copley Square.
Parking: Meter.
Picnicking: Yes.
Rest Rooms: No.

PAUL REVERE HOUSE
19 North Square, Boston, MA 02113
(617) 523-2338

FUN SCALE

"Listen my children, and you shall hear / of the midnight ride of Paul Revere..."
Find out what life was like around the time of the famous midnight ride, when Paul Revere went galloping through Middlesex county to warn the farmers and villagers that the British were coming. Take a self-guided tour through the house where, at one time or another, Revere, one of his wives, and his sixteen children lived. Point out the simple and rustic kitchen and the bumpy beds, and ask your kids to imagine living in the close quarters of this seventeenth and eighteenth century house—with fifteen brothers and sisters! I'll bet they'll never complain about having to share the bathroom again!

Age range: Kids 2-4 no; for kids 5-7, nothing is hands-on, but they might enjoy seeing a piece of Boston's history; kids 8 and up, yes.
Hours: November 1 through April 14, daily from 9:30 a.m. to 4:15 p.m.
April 15 through October 31, from 9:30 a.m. to 5:15 p.m.
Admission: Adults $2.50, seniors and students $2.00, children (5-17) $1.00.
Time Allowance: 20 to 30 minutes.
Directions: Via the "T," take the Green or Orange Line to Haymarket Station. By foot, follow the Freedom Trail's red stripe on the sidewalks of the North End. The house is five minutes from Faneuil Hall and Quincy Market.
Parking: Meter and pay-lot.
Wheelchair Accessible: First floor only.
Restaurant: No, but nearby.
Picnicking: No, but nearby.
Rest Rooms: Yes.
Gift Shop: Yes; T-shirts, postcards, books, notecards.

45

FRANKLIN PARK ZOO
Franklin Park
Boston, MA 02121
(617) 442-2002

FUN SCALE

Boston's seventy two-acre suburban zoo, opened in 1913 in the center of a five hundred-acre park in Dorchester, is a safe yet wild place to explore. Walk through the eight fluted columns of granite into a micro world of tropical, desert, and forest delights.

To begin with, visit the five-acre **Children's Zoo**, located not far from the entrance. There you'll find the reptile and amphibian building, where a long snake mural winds around corners past the tanks of the Rosy boa, California king snake, and ring-tailed geckoes. Then walk outside to the **Petting Zoo** and make the acquaintance of some New England farm animals, including sheep, geese, cows, and petite pigs. There are even some endangered spotted and polka-dotted chickens. Stroll past the porcupine and coyote. Warning: Not part of the **Petting Zoo**!

Kids will also enjoy the twelve-acre **Hooves and Horns** division. Wildebeest and zebras, dromedaries and ostriches, roam or graze in their fenced enclosures. If someone in your family has never seen a real zebra, he or she is in for a treat. What a beautiful animal!

The popular **African Tropical Forest** is an impressively realistic three-acre complex. Imitating the heat, humidity, and landscape of Equatorial Africa, the exhibit's

creators have provided a realistic natural environment for the animals while educating and delighting their human visitors. The animals climb, slither, fly, and forage in their created habitats. Most admired, perhaps, are the lowland gorillas, which have free access to both the indoor and outdoor environments. There are many other creatures as well. The warthogs (considered by some to be the ugliest creatures on Earth) are often visible but take a midday siesta, as do many of the diurnal rainforest beasts. The hippo can be viewed both from ground level and through a water tank below ground. And don't forget to admire the spirally twisted horns of the endangered North African addax, or the arresting features of the mandrill, a large, fierce baboon with a colorful Sigmund Freud-style goatee.

At the other side of the zoo is **Bird's World**, a seven-acre complex that includes a flight cage, waterfowl pond, and oriental bird house. Ascend to the elevated walkway of the flight cage for a bird's-eye view of the birds. It's a heady experience. In all, **Bird's World** is host to 101 species, including cormorants, macaws, and the amazing Motmot, whose tail looks like the feathers on a dart. Or is it the other way around? If you're out at Franklin Park, this exhibit is a must.

Also available at Franklin Park is **City Mini-Golf**, a miniature golf course set up by the Children's Museum of Boston. For a fee of $2.00 for adults and $1.00 for kids, you can play a round of nine holes before continuing on your journey.

A final note: For those who are wondering about the neighborhood, there has been no record of any incidence of crime either in the zoo or in the surrounding park. The zoo is a friendly and exciting place to spend an afternoon or morning, especially in warm weather.

Age Range: Any age enjoys a zoo.
Hours: Summer, daily from 9:00 a.m. to 5:00 p.m. Winter, daily from 9:00 a.m. to 4:00 p.m.
Admission: Adults (ages 12+) $5.00, kids (4-11) and seniors $2.50.
Time Allowance: 1 to 3 hours.
Directions: Via the "T," take the Orange Line to the Forest Hills stop and hop on a bus to the zoo, or take a 15-minute walk.
Parking: Free.
Wheelchair Accessible: Yes.
Restaurant: Yes, snack bar.
Picnicking: Yes.
Rest Rooms: Yes.
Gift Shop: Yes; T-shirts, stuffed animals, postcards.

KIDPORT
Terminal C, Logan Airport
Boston
(617) 561-1600

FUN SCALE

Terminal C is the place to be when you're hanging around Logan Airport with kids. It offers several cool, kid-friendly activities.

Three words—"Kids," "Here," and "Please"—are scrawled across the glass panels as you enter the Kidport area, a free play area run by Massport in cooperation with The Children's Museum. It's designed to offer a break from the emotional experiences caused by issues of anticipation, excitement, and someone's coming or going. Whether you're waiting to pick up or drop off, or whether you're just venturing on a

family safari, Kidport provides a perfect intermission from the day's activities. What could be better than a play space with a giant car, plane, train, and rocket, all with a view of busy aircraft activity in the background?

Don't forget to experiment with the **What's New in New England** TV screens. The touch-activated monitors describe various events in New England by pushing options like "Adventure," "Brainpower," and "Arts."

Take some time to look at the sculptures in the main hall. Two fascinating gravity-loaded, kinetic sculptures in the lobby provide endless hours of visual entertainment, as moving parts bounce, splat, swirl, sproinng, roll, and gyrate! Beware though: There's always the

danger of becoming so engulfed that you miss your connection. Good luck tearing your child away!

Before you leave, check out the wild mirror pieces on the wall near the **Marbleworks**. All of a sudden you're fragmented into hundreds of shapes and distortions. What an illusion!

For helpful information on transporting unaccompanied minors, and tips on flying with toddlers and teens, Massport puts out a guide called *When Kids Fly*. It's free and can be obtained by calling (617)973-5600.

Age Range: 2-7 yes; 8 and up, no for the Kidport, but might appreciate the touch-activated TV screens. Everyone likes the kinetic sculptures.
Hours: Always open.
Admission: Free.
Time Allowance: Depends on layover time.
Directions: Via the "T," take the Blue Line to the Airport Stop. Hop on the shuttle bus to Terminal C.
Parking: Pay-lot.
Wheelchair Accessible: Yes.
Restaurant: Yes, several surrounding.
Picnicking: Yes.
Rest Rooms: Yes.
Gift Shop: Yes, close by.

BOSTON BY LITTLE FEET
77 North Washington Street
Boston, MA 02114
(617) 367-2345

FUN SCALE 🎈🎈🎈🎈

For a kid-oriented walking tour of historical Boston, hook up with Boston by Little Feet in front of Faneuil Hall, at the Samuel Adams statue on Congress Street. The action-packed and fun-filled tour lasts for an hour and covers ten historical sites, ranging from Faneuil Hall to the Fleet Bank. Young walkers must be between six and twelve years, and must be accompanied by an adult.

Age Range: 6-12, accompanied by an adult.
Hours: From May 1 to October 31, Saturdays at 10:00 a.m., Sundays at 2:00 p.m.
Time Allowance: About an hour.
Directions: Via the "T," take the Blue Line to State Street.
Parking: Meter and pay-lot.

50

COOL "T" STOPS
All on the Red Line

FUN SCALE

Some of the more fun "T" stops can be found at **Porter Square, Kendall Square,** and **Broadway** stations. Okay, there's no need to go completely out of your way; but if you do happen to find yourself at one of these places, check it out.

Porter Square has what has got to be one of the longest, steepest escalators on this planet. Go on, have a ride—it's free! Just make sure everyone's holding on. To make the escalator experience even more elevating, have a look at the sculptures fastened on the metal strip between the two escalators. They're cast-metal versions of gloves and other articles of clothing left behind by hurried commuters. Watch these odd creations whiz by as you go up and down, which you might want to do several times, given the awesomeness of the ride. At the top, step outside and look up at the giant kinetic sculpture moving gently in the breeze.

At the **Broadway** stop practical object sculptures by Jay Coogan adorn the plain white walls. A shovel, a clothes iron—is it art? How silly! Downstairs, clay tiles made by kids are plastered into the walls next to the tracks.

Kendall Station is the home of "The Kendall Band." Okay, it's not exactly a band in the conventional sense, but it does produce spectacular sounds. Swing the designated handle slowly but firmly back and forth to activate the pipes. The giant long metal tubes dangling in between the tracks will begin to sway back and forth, creating a magnificently loud melody as the hammers sound the bells. Don't give up if it doesn't work the first time. Sometimes it takes a while to get the rhythm of the handle. Afterward, step outside and have a look at the sculpture in the plaza across the street.

It's a shiny bronze globe with a fountain spraying from its periphery. A nice example of the integration of art with urban design. Besides, every kid likes a fountain.

Directions: Check your nearest "T" station for a map.
Wheelchair Accessible: Yes.

DR.PAUL DUDLEY WHITE
CHARLES RIVER BIKE PATH
from Watertown Square to
Museum of Science, Boston

FUN SCALE

If you're looking for a scenic and fairly well-kept bike path, try the one that spans a distance of seventeen miles round trip. It runs along both sides of the Charles River between the Galen Street Bridge in Watertown and the River Street Bridge in Boston. The bikeway runs from the Museum of Science through the Esplanade to Watertown Square, and back along the Cambridge side of the river on both sides of Memorial Drive, returning to the Museum of Science. The path is also open to joggers, walkers, strollers, and roller-bladers, and no, it's not mandatory to do the entire seventeen miles of the course. Nice for family outings.

ARNOLD ARBORETUM
OF HARVARD UNIVERSITY
125 Arborway, Jamaica Plain, MA 02130
(617) 524-1718

FUN SCALE

A magnificent open space located incredibly close to the center of Boston, the Arnold Arboretum consists of a 265-acre site designed by Frederick Law Olmstead, the same landscape architect who designed Central Park in New York City. It contains more than seven thousand kinds of woody plants perfect for this climatic zone (most are labeled by genus and species).

The changes in plant life from season to season are dramatic. Follow the winding pathways past cork trees, sunflower meadows, fantastic silk trees, and much more. You can go on foot, by bike, or on roller blades, according to preference.

Oh, and don't forget to take advantage of some of the many organized activities for kids designed to complement school programs.

Age Range: Any age.
Hours: Dawn to dusk, 365 days a year.
Admission: Free.
Time Allowance: No set time.
Directions: Via the "T," take the Orange Line to Forest Hills. Exit and turn right up South Street. It's a five-minute walk.
Parking: Plentiful and free.
Wheelchair Accessible: Yes.
Restaurant: No.
Picnicking: Yes.
Rest Rooms: Yes.
Gift Shop: No.

CAMBRIDGE

HARVARD UNIVERSITY
MUSEUMS OF NATURAL HISTORY
26 Oxford Street, Cambridge, MA 02138
(617) 495-2248

FUN SCALE

The Harvard Museum has four divisions: the **Botanical Museum**, the **Mineralogical and Geological Museum**, the **Museum of Comparative Zoology**, and the **Peabody Museum of Archaeology and Ethnology**. Packing the whole thing into a single visit might be a bit much for small kids, but they can select and drag their parents toward what interests them.

The **Botanical Museum** houses the world-famous Glass Flowers exhibit. At the turn of the century, a German father and son team constructed over three thousand botanical models entirely of glass, using a special technique whose secret has been lost. Examine the incredibly realistic-looking flowers, fruit, and insects. Even the mold and blight on the plant specimens are made of glass. The objects were created to instruct, not merely to adorn.

In the **Mineralogical and Geological Museum** you'll see amazing rock specimens, such as gypsum, which looks like porcupine quills, byssolite, which is grayish-green and hairy, and hematite, appropriately nicknamed "kidney ore" for its smooth, bulbous shape.

Take a look at the many stuffed animals and other samples in the **Museum of Comparative Zoology**. Their collection includes crocodiles, an African warthog, a giant 7-foot 10-inch fresh-water turtle shell, and even a mastadon, to name just a few. Don't forget to push the buttons and hear the sounds of seals and dolphins, and the deep, eerie calls of whales.

In the **Peabody Museum** you'll find "The Hall of the Maya" and other rotating

programs. Learn to understand the people of the past from the artifacts that have survived them.

Age Range: For kids 2-4, it's not a hands-on situation, but they might enjoy looking at an abbreviated version; kids 5 and up yes.
Hours: Monday through Saturday from 9:00 a.m. to 4:30 p.m., Sunday from 1:00 to 4:30 p.m.
Admission: Adults $4.00, seniors and students $3.00, children (3-13) $1.00.
Directions: Via the "T," take the Red Line to Harvard Square. Walk through Harvard Yard, past Memorial Hall, to Oxford Street. The museum is on the right.
Parking: Free lot on weekends; otherwise meter.
Wheelchair Accessible: Yes.
Restaurant: No, but close by.
Picnicking: No, but close by.
Rest Rooms: Yes.
Gift Shop: Yes; fabulous T-shirts, minerals, animal tattoos and calendars.

CAMBRIDGESIDE GALLERIA
100 Cambridgeside Place
Cambridge, MA 02141
(617) 621-8666

FUN SCALE

The new and architecturally enticing Cambridgeside Galleria is the site of hordes of shops, eateries, and the Sports Museum. The shops range from Baby Gap and Gap Kids to Kaybee Toys. In the Food Court there are eating stands with a multitude of choices. Get a cookie at Original Cookies or expand your eating culture at Au Bon Pain or The Cajun Big Easy.

Hours: Monday through Saturday from 10:00 a.m. to 9:30 p.m., Sunday from noon to 6:00 p.m.
Directions: Via the "T," take the Green Line to the Lechmere stop and it's across the street.
Parking: Meter and pay-lot.
Wheelchair Accessible: Yes.
Restaurant: Yes, many.
Picnicking: Yes.
Rest Rooms: Yes.

THE SPORTS MUSEUM OF NEW ENGLAND
Cambridgeside Galleria, 100 Cambridgeside Place, Cambridge, MA 02141
(617) 57-SPORT

FUN SCALE

New England has contributed tremendously to sports history. It's a tradition worth preserving and celebrating. The Sports Museum of New England does just that and in grand style.

Located in the Cambridgeside Galleria, the museum houses major sports displays and fun interactive exhibits. As you enter, for instance, you'll be greeted by a Formula One race car that was driven and owned by Paul Newman. Sidle up to a true-to-life sculpture of Larry Bird, Bobby Orr, or Carl Yastremski, or

check out the exhibit of Candlepin Bowling, a sport unique to New England. Among the interactive exhibits is a simulated game of catch with pitcher Roger Clemens; another exhibit demonstrates the challenge of competing in the wheelchair division of the Boston Marathon by giving you a chance to operate a wheelchair in a simulated race along the Charles River.

Educational and fun, the Sports Museum of New England is worth a visit.

Age Range: For kids 2-4, there's probably not much value; for ages 5 and up, anyone who's a sports fan will enjoy this experience.

Hours: Sunday from twelve noon to 6:00 p.m., Monday through Saturday from 10:00 a.m. to 9:30 p.m.

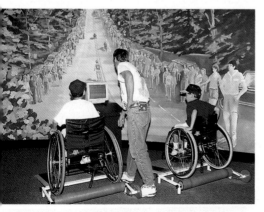

Admission: Adults and Children (8 and up) $6.00, seniors and children (4-7) $4.50.

Time Allowance: 1-2 hours.

Directions: Via the "T," take the Green Line to the Lechmere stop. Enter the Cambridgeside Galleria and go to the first floor.

Parking: Meter and pay-lot.

Wheelchair Accessible: Yes.

Restaurant: No, but nearby.

Picnicking: No.

Rest Rooms: No, but nearby.

Gift Shop: Yes; T-shirts and other sporty paraphernalia.

57

THE MIT MUSEUM
265 Massachusetts Avenue
Cambridge, MA 02139
(617) 253-4444

FUN SCALE

Amazing, mind-blowing, and ultra-cool—that's the Massachusetts Institute of Technology (MIT) museum. It's not as huge as some of the other museums, but it's full of fun hands-on exhibits.

It starts with a computer, of course: You can plug into the history of MIT or into a map of the exhibits. Of these, one of the most spectacular is **Bill Parker's Light Sculptures**. The plasma globes shoot/spit out rays and splotches of light inside hand blown glass globes. Touch the outside and see how the effect of the heat from your hand affects the color and light. Wild!

See whether you can figure out what makes a hologram work. The MIT Museum houses the largest and most comprehensive collection of holography in the *world*, including scientific, medical, technical, and artistic imaging. Look at the turbulent "Smoke Plume" and the realistic "Still Life," to name only a couple.

One room is called **Mathspace**. Inside you can explore the theme of geometry by tinkering with the museum's collection of math toys.

Don't miss the Harold Edgerton exhibit, appropriately called **Stopping Time**. Fascinating photographs of

58

frozen motion decorate the walls. Watch the video first, then move on to images of a giant drop of milk, a balloon exploding, water running, and a strobe photo of an owl in light. Each is frozen in motion.

The MIT Museum is definitely worth a visit. It's a great way to learn something about the merging of art and science, and it's painless!

Age Range: Kids 2-4 will be visually captivated for a short visit; 5-7 will enjoy the lights and colors and the Mathspace; kids 8 and up will definitely enjoy the museum.

Hours: Open year-round Tuesday through Friday from 9:00 a.m. to 5:00 p.m.; Saturday and Sunday from 1:00 p.m. to 5:00 p.m.

Admission: Donations of $2.00 for adults, $1.00 for kids.

Time allowance: About an hour.

Directions: Via the "T," take the Red Line to Central Square and walk down Massachusetts Avenue toward the Boston skyline. The museum is on the left side.

Parking: Meter and pay-lot.

Wheelchair Accessible: Yes.

Restaurant: Not in museum, but within walking distance.

Picnicking: No.

Rest rooms: Yes.

Gift shop: Yes; holograms, games, MIT bags, time pyramids, gyro walkers, sound sensor plasma globes, and even paper airplane kits.

CHARLES RIVERBOAT TOURS
100 Cambridgeside Place, Suite 320, Cambridge, MA 02141
(617) 621-3000

FUN SCALE

Passing through the canal and out to the Charles River, the traditional riverboats take you on a fifty-minute narrated tour and pleasure cruise. After a quick stop at the Museum of Science to pick up passengers, the cruise begins. Passing under the Longfellow Bridge, appropriately known as the "salt and pepper shaker" bridge because of its distinctive structures, the riverboat takes you on a river's-eye view of Boston and Cambridge, including historic Beacon Hill, the Esplanade, MIT, and Harvard University. Sit back and enjoy as the crew teams glide past in their shells, intent on their oars. This is a unique way to experience the Boston riverscape.

Age Range: Kids 2 and up yes; walking around is allowed.
Hours: June through August from 12:00 noon to 5:00 p.m., on the hour. September/October and April/May, weekends only from 12:00 noon to 5:00 p.m., on the hour.
Admission: Adults $7.00, seniors $6.00, children (12 and under) $5.00.
Time Allowance: 50 minutes.
Directions: Via the "T," take the Green Line to the Lechmere stop. Walk through the Cambridgeside Galleria and out to the canal.
Parking: Pay-lot and garage.
Wheelchair Accessible: Yes.
Restaurant: Yes, snacks, except on Riverboat Dinner or Luncheon Cruises.
Picnicking: Yes.
Rest Rooms: Yes.
Gift Shop: No.

CAMBRIDGE COMMON PLAYGROUND
Garden and Waterhouse Streets
Cambridge

FUN SCALE

Rumor has it that this playground is "the best around." At least, that's the hands-down opinion of the adults I met escorting kids from toddlers to six- or seven-year-olds. It's a fenced-in play space nestled among the trees of the spacious Cambridge Common. The space is filled with a variety of play structures, from chutes and ladders to jungle gyms and swings. Shady trees provide relief from the summer heat, and there are benches, picnic tables, and a drinking fountain. The Common has space for Frisbee throwing and even kite flying, if there's no ball game on.

Directions: Via the "T," take the Red Line to Harvard Square. Follow the Church Street exit signs out of the subway, turn right, and go up Massachusetts Avenue. to the Common (corner of Massachusetts Avenue and Garden Street). The playground is on the other side of the Common.
Parking: Meter.
Restaurant: No, but within walking distance.
Picnicking: Yes.
Rest Rooms: No.

AUBURNDALE PARK
West Pine Street
Auburndale, MA 02166

FUN SCALE

Auburndale Park, on the bank of the Charles River, is a wonderful place to pass a spring or summer's day. Bring a picnic basket with some grillables: There are barbecue pits in the **James "Chub" Ryan Picnic Area**. After you spread out the blanket and set up camp, there are many options from which to choose.

If sports is your bag, there are tennis and basketball courts, baseball fields, and volleyball nets. The playground equipment is fantastic— swing sets, spinning dishes, wooden climbers, fish swings, seesaws, and horse shoes. And of course there's always the pastoral setting of the Charles River, blue and sparkling and lined with overhanging trees. With the quacking ducks and occasional boats skimming by, the Charles is a romantic's paradise.

Speaking of boats, you might consider renting a canoe from the Charles River Canoe and Kayak Center(see below) one mile upriver. Pile into the canoe—each one holds from three to five people—and float down to the park. Tie the canoe to a tree, spend a couple of hours at the Auburndale Park, and paddle back. What a way to spend the day!

There's ice skating on the Charles in the winter.

Directions (4 miles from Boston): Take Commonwealth Avenue (Rt. 30) through Auburndale Square to the second set of lights. Turn right on Melrose and take your second left on West Pine Street.
Parking: Free and ample.
Restaurant: No.
Picnicking: Yes; with barbecue pits.
Rest Rooms: No.

BUNKER HILL PAVILION
55 Constitution Road
Charlestown, MA 02129
(617) 241-7575

FUN SCALE 🎈🎈🎈🎈

The Battle of Bunker Hill was the first major battle of the Revolutionary War. (The battle actually took place on Breed's Hill, but why quibble?) For those in the mood for a dose of American history, the battle site today is experienced in two parts, the pavilion and the monument. You might begin at the Bunker Hill Pavilion with "The Whites of Their Eyes," a multimedia presentation in the wrap-around theater based on the Battle of Bunker Hill and the events leading up to the bloody confrontation. An actor playing the role of Paul Revere presents a dramatic narration of the story.

Age Range: 2-4 no; 5-7 possibly; 8 and up yes.
Hours: Daily from 9:00 a.m. to 4:00 p.m., July and August until 5:00 p.m.
Admission: $2.00 per person.
Time Allowance: 30 minutes.
Directions: One possibility would be to take a water shuttle from the Long Wharf Pier to the Navy Yard. They run regularly, and at $1.00 a ride they're a true bargain.
Parking: Free lots.
Wheelchair Accessible: Yes.
Restaurant: No.
Picnicking: Yes.
Rest Rooms: Yes.
Gift Shop: Yes; postcards, books.

BUNKER HILL MONUMENT

Monument Avenue
Charlestown, MA 02129
(617) 242-5641

FUN SCALE

Copyright © Raytheon Publication Department

Follow the multimedia presentation at the Bunker Hill Pavilion with a ten-minute walk over to the Bunker Hill Monument. Dioramas line the walls of the lodge at the foot of the monument. Check them out. They illustrate the famous battle, and although they're not as exciting as "The Whites of Their Eyes" exhibit, the dioramas may provide those less energetic souls with some entertainment while the kids sprint up the steps of the monument.

The monument (Bunker Hill, itself, is actually a mile or so away) stands on the actual site of the famous battle. The 221-foot, 294-step granite memorial provides a fantastic panoramic view of the harbor—to say nothing of the aerobic climb up and back! Maybe the kids will go to bed early tonight.

Age Range: 2-4 doubtful; 5-7 might enjoy the climb; 8 and up yes.
Hours: Daily from 9:00 a.m. to 5:00 p.m., with 4:30 as the last monument ascent.
Admission: Free.
Time Allowance: About an hour.
Directions: Via the "T," take the Orange Line to Community College.
Parking: Free street spaces, but watch out for street sweepers.
Wheelchair Accessible: The lodge is but the monument is not.
Restaurant: No, but within walking distance.
Picnicking: Yes.
Rest Rooms: Yes.
Gift Shop: Summer only; books, toy fifes, musket balls, postcards.

U.S.S.CONSTITUTION SHIP AND MUSEUM

P.O. Box 1812, Charlestown Navy Yard
Boston, MA 02129
(617) 426-1812

FUN SCALE

The U.S.S. *Constitution*, or "Old Ironsides," resides in the Charlestown Navy Yard as a currently commissioned U.S. Navy ship. First launched in 1797, the frigate is loaded with American history, from fending off pirate attacks to fighting the British in the War of 1812. She is the oldest commissioned warship in the world.

Take a tour with a sailor clad in an 1812 uniform, and learn about life at sea during those difficult times. Look at the cannons on deck; go below and experience the close quarters endured by the crews of yesterday. With such conditions, it's no wonder the ship carried eight thousand gallons of rum!

The twenty-five minute tour is well worth the price of admission, but be forewarned that lines are long in the summer unless you get there early in the morning.

The U.S.S. *Constitution* Museum is located next to the ship and provides a hands-on approach to learning about life at sea. The interactive exhibits include knot tying, sleeping in hammocks, raising a sail, and pretending to be a captain through a simulated computer game.

Age Range: Kids 2-4 doubtful; 5 and up yes.
Hours: Summer, daily from 9:00 a.m. to 6:00 p.m.; winter, daily from 9:00 a.m. to 4:00 p.m.
Spring and fall, daily from 9:00 a.m. to 5:00 p.m.
Admission: Adults $3.00, seniors $2.00, kids (6-16) $1.50.
Time Allowance: About an hour for both.
Directions: Via the "T," take the Green Line to North Station and walk across the bridge (a ten minute walk).

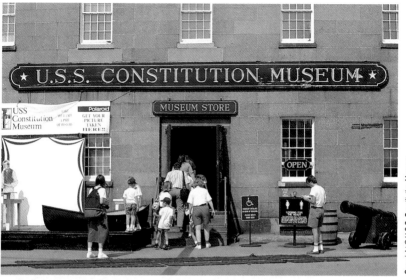

or take the ferry from long wharf.
Parking: Meter and pay-lot.
Wheelchair Accessible: Yes.
Restaurant: No, but within walking distance.
Picnicking: No, but within walking distance.
Rest Rooms: Yes, in museum.
Gift Shop: Yes; mugs, T-shirts, calendars.

PUPPET SHOWPLACE THEATER
32-33 Station Street
Brookline, MA 02146
(617) 731-6400

FUN SCALE

For a fun weekend event, catch a puppet show in Brookline Village, where the magic and fantasy of theater and children's literature come together.

The puppet shows, imaginatively performed by professional puppeteers, take the audience through Aesop's fables, ethnic lore, and folk and fairy tales from around the world. The element of audience participation and narration, both before and after, allows the kids to realize that puppets are puppets and not to be feared. It's a delightfully "kid-friendly" environment and well worth a visit.

Age Range: Children 2-4 may be too squirmy to sit through the whole performance; best for those 5 and up, especially 5-8.

Hours: During the school year, Saturday and Sunday 1:00 p.m. and 3:00 p.m. performances. School vacation times, 1:00 p.m. and 3:00 p.m. daily. Summer hours, 11:00 a.m. and 1:00 p.m. daily. On the first Thursday of each month there's a Tot Show for preschoolers at 10:30 a.m.

Admission: $5.00.

Time Allowance: 45 minutes.

Directions: Via the "T," go to Brookline Village on the Riverside Green Line. Cross the street and you're there.

Parking: Meter and pay-lot.

Wheelchair Accessible: Yes.

Restaurant: Not in theatre, but within easy walking distance.

Picnicking: No.

Rest Rooms: Yes.

Gift Shop: Yes; postcards, T-shirts, puppets.

MUSEUM OF TRANSPORTATION
15 Newton Street
Brookline, MA 02146
(617) 522-6140

FUN SCALE

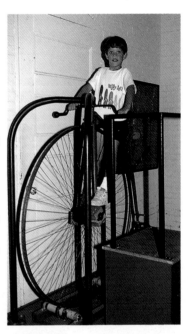

An 1888 carriage house situated in Lars Anderson Park houses The Museum of Transportation. Autos of all vintages are on display in the open inner courtyard, and the display changes on an annual basis.

Downstairs you'll find the area of permanent exhibits, including prized motorcars, antique autos, and a turn-of-the-century trolley car. At the **Inventors' Workshop,** kids can build their own prototype car of the future from recycled objects. Moving along to **The Children's Activity Center,** climb on the Volkswagen dune buggy. Test your strength on an antique gas pump or examine the mechanics of a Thunderbird engine. Mount the police motorcycle with sidecar and let your imagination roll!

Age Range: Kids 2-4, possibly downstairs in the interactive area; 5 and up yes, if interested in automobiles.

Hours: Wednesday through Sunday from 10:00 a.m. to 5:00 p.m.

Admission: Adults $4.00; students, seniors, and children 3 and over $2.00.

Time Allowance: About an hour.
Directions: Via the " T," take the Green Line to Cleveland Circle and catch Bus #51 (Wednesday through Saturday).
Parking: Free and plentiful.
Wheelchair Accessible: Yes.
Restaurant: No.
Picnicking: Yes, at the pavilion close by.
Rest Rooms: Yes.
Gift Shop: Yes; T-shirts, hats, books, model cars.

ALLANDALE FARM
259 Allandale Road
Brookline, MA
(617) 524-1531

FUN SCALE

On a leisurely stroll through Allandale Farm, you will see bunnies, chickens, an occasional cow, luscious gardens, and apple trees drooping with fruit. Stop and watch apples being squished and turned into cider in the apple press. Walk through the extensive vegetable and flower gardens. Can you identify which flowers are edible? Pass through the farm stand afterward. You're bound to leave Allandale Farm with a good taste in your mouth.

Age Range: Any age.
Hours: May 1 through Christmas Eve from 10:00 a.m. to 6:00 p.m.
Admission: Free.
Time Allowance: About an hour.
Directions: From Boston, drive on Jamaicaway to the end, which leads to Rt. 1 South. Follow Rt. 1 South to the top of the hill (Faulkner Hospital will be on your right, just before Allandale Street), and turn right on Allandale Street. The farm is half a mile down on your right.
Parking: Free and ample.
Wheelchair Accessible: Everything is on one level, but sections are bumpy.
Restaurant: No.
Picnicking: Yes, with permission.
Rest Rooms: Yes.
Gift Shop: Tons of fresh vegetables, cider, lollipops, and honey.

KIDSPACE
The Atrium Mall
300 Boylston Street, Chestnut Hill, MA 02167
(617) 527-1400

FUN SCALE

Nobody ever claimed that shopping with toddlers was easy. The Atrium Mall in Chestnut Hill provides relief with the Kidspace. It's a *free* play space for kids (best for toddlers and younger). There's no attendant or baby sitter, but it does provide your kids with a great break from being dragged around to the many upscale shops in the mall. Plan to stay with your child or trade off with one of the parents in the Kidspace. It's a safe environment with the advantages of a changing room, a telephone room, and bathrooms. The carpeted floor provides a comfortable surface for kids to scoot about and play in the plastic castles and cars.

Age Range: Best for kids 6 and younger.
Hours: Monday through Saturday from 10:00 a.m. to 9:30 p.m., Sunday from 12:00 noon to 6:00 p.m.
Admission: Free.
Directions (5 miles from Boston): Take Rt. 9 to Chestnut Hill. The mall is a large, impressive atrium building on the left.
Parking: Underground lot.
Wheelchair Accessible: Yes.
Restaurant: Many.
Picnicking: Yes.
Rest Rooms: Yes, with changing tables.

BLUE HILLS TRAILSIDE
MUSEUM AND RESERVATION
1904 Canton Avenue, Milton, MA 02186
(617) 333-0690

FUN SCALE

Located just a few miles outside of Boston, these 6,500 acres of unspoiled reservation land offer something that's increasingly hard to find: nature. Forget the hustle and bustle of city life and come for a peaceful walk among the Blue Hills—or browse in the museum and learn something about the natural history of the area.

For those who plan to do both, the Trailside Museum is a good starting point for your Blue Hills experience. Changing interactive exhibits focus on the natural and cultural history of the reservation. Climb up into the viewing tower and look for hawks. Enter a Native American wigwam and feel the deerskins. Check out the honeybees in the giant observation hive.

Every month has its own special event. October features **Gone Batty**, in which facts and lore about bats are explored and some myths exploded. In January it's **Owl Events.** Sign up for a lantern-lit owl prowl. Sounds spooky!

Outside is where the live action is. Reach through the fence and pat the deer if you like, but leave the bobcat alone! For more energetic souls, a hike up the mesh of trails will be rewarded by a spectacular panoramic view of Blue Hills. This is a great way to spend a family outing. Don't forget your lunch!

Age Range: Between the museum and the reservation, there's something for everyone.
Hours: Museum hours are Wednesday through Sunday from 10:00 a.m. to 5:00 p.m. Open Mondays on state holidays.
Admission: Adults $3.00, children (3-15) $1.50, seniors $2.00.

Time Allowance: 1 or 2 hours.
Directions (5 miles from Boston): Take Rt. 128 (93) to Exit 2B (Milton), to Rt. 138 North. The parking lot is another half mile on your right.
Parking: Free.
Wheelchair Accessible: Yes.
Restaurant: No, but within a mile there's a Ho Jo's.
Picnicking: Yes.
Rest Rooms: Yes.
Gift Shop: Yes; puppets, bird feeders, books.

72

FOREST RIVER PARK
Clifton Avenue, Salem
MA 01970
(508) 744-0180

FUN SCALE

Overlooking Salem's harbor lie twenty-nine acres of park land including two beaches, a playground, and a salt-water pool. The beaches have lifeguards during the summer hours.

The playground features a variety of swinging/ climbing/bouncing equipment, along with a *steep* slide popular with the big kids. Take a piece of an old cardboard box. Climb to the top, sit down, and let go. Whee! Heartstopping.

The pool is an unusual attraction. It contains salt water instead of chlorinated fresh water . Sort of like ocean swimming minus the waves. Try it!

Hours: 8:00 a.m. to 8:00 p.m.

Directions (15 miles from Boston): Take Rt. 1A North to Salem State University and continue straight on West Avenue to the end.

Parking: Nonresident parking during the week in the summer costs $4.00. Weekend parking is for residents only and costs $4.00.

Restaurant: No.

Picnicking: Yes.

Rest Rooms: Yes, with showers.

PEABODY ESSEX MUSEUM
East India Square
Salem, MA 01970
(508) 745-9500

FUN SCALE

The Peabody Museum and The Essex Institute merged in 1992 to form The Peabody Essex Museum. Their merging united a maritime-oriented museum and an institute dedicated to preserving the culture of Essex county. The Peabody half was founded by sea captains in 1799 as the storehouse for artifacts, curiosities, and navigational information gathered from around the world. The museum today contains collections of maritime history and art, Asian export art, archaeology, and natural history. The Essex half is a regional museum that collects, preserves, and interprets the history and culture of Essex County from the seventeenth century to the present day.

The Peabody section, which may be more fun for kids, is loaded with historical nautical paraphernalia. Nothing is hands-on, but the floor is carpeted and the atmosphere is light, providing a cheerful environment for looking. One gallery is full of exciting bowsprit carvings: Check out the mermaids! Marvel at the giant jaw bone of a whale. Some of the most interesting rooms display provisions from sailing voyages of bygone times. Note the jars of coffee beans from the eighteenth century, white with age. (What wouldn't be after sitting in a jar for two hundred years?)

The Essex section is less of a "kid environment," but contains some important memorabilia. In addition to a large library, there's a gallery of American furniture, silver,

74

...nd portraits. Peek into the room with toys, dolls, and games.

Age Range: Kids 2-4 no; 5-7 probably; 8 and up yes.

Hours: Monday through Saturday from 10:00 a.m. to 5:00 p.m., Sunday from 12:00 noon to 5:00 p.m.

Admission: Galleries and Libraries OR Historic Houses:
Adults $6.00, seniors $5.00, kids $3.50.
Galleries, Libraries, AND Historic Houses:
Adults $10.00, seniors $8.50, kids $6.00.
Free admission on the first Thursday of the month from 5:00 to 8:00 p.m.

Time Allowance: 1 to 3 hours.

Directions (15 miles from Boston): Take Rt. 1 North to Rt. 128 North and get off at Exit 26, Lowell Street, Peabody. Drive 2.4 miles and turn left after Dunkin' Donuts onto Bridge Street (Rt. 107). Proceed 1.2 miles to Winter Street (1-A), turn right, and follow 1-A past Salem Common (on left) to Essex Street. Take a right and you're there.

Parking: Yes, meter and pay-lot.

Wheelchair Accessible: Mostly.

Restaurant: No, but within an easy walk.

Picnicking: No, but within an easy walk.

Rest Rooms: Yes.

Gift Shop: Yes; jewelry, folk crafts, books, and prints.

TOT STOP
41 Foster Street, Arlington, MA 02174
(617) 643-8687

Museum Place, Salem, MA 01970
(508) 741-5704

FUN SCALE

There are two Tot Stops: one in Arlington and one in Salem. Each has a different feel, but they share the same kid-play philosophy. The Arlington Tot Stop is housed in the auditorium of an old junior high school, which may sound rustic but really isn't. The Salem Tot Stop is located in a new mall-type shopping center.

The pay-to-play situation offers a safe, clean, and friendly atmosphere where children can be children surrounded by a multitude of toys and play paraphernalia. Parents have the option of either playing with their kids or allowing them to frolic with the others. There are also books and magazines for parents to read over a cup of coffee.

Age Range: 2-6.
Hours: Monday through Saturday from 9:30 a.m. to 5:30 p.m., Fridays (pizza night) in Arlington open until 8:00 p.m. Thursdays (pizza night) in Salem open until 8:00 p.m. Salem is also open Sunday.
Admission: Parents, and siblings under 10 months, are free. Children $5.50, babies under 10 months (without a sibling) $2.00. Family maximum $12.95. There are other package deals available; call for

formation.

me Allowance: 1 1/2 to 3 hours, or until one of you gets over stimulated.

rections:

lington site (7 miles from Boston)—Go north on Massachusetts Avenue. A few blocks before entering lington Center, take a right on Foster Street, then a left into the parking lot. Tot Stop is on Tufts Street on e other side of the lot; look for a large brick building on your right.

alem site (15 miles from Boston)— Follow Rt. 128 North to Exit 26 (114 East). Follow 114 East into Salem Rt. 107 toward Beverly. Go straight through the rotary and, just beyond it, take the first right. Ahead is the useum Place.

arking: Arlington site—free. Salem site—pay-lot (50¢ per hour, first half hour free).

heelchair Accessible: Yes.

estaurant: Snacks.

cnicking: No.

est Rooms: Yes, with changing tables.

ft Shop: No.

THE HOUSE OF SEVEN GABLES
54 Turner Street
Salem, MA 01970
(508) 744-0991

FUN SCALE

Come see the site of inspiration for Nathaniel Hawthorne's classic 1851 novel. The seventeenth-century mansion is surrounded by a complex of early houses and elegant gardens on Salem's waterfront, among them Hawthorne's birthplace. The guided tours provide answers to all kinds of questions about life during the seventeenth century. Visit the eighteenth-century counting house and nineteenth-century gardens. This trip probably won't be much fun for the younger folk, but might fascinate older children and their parents. Check it out.

Age Range: Kids 2-7 no; 8 and up possibly or definitely if interested in history.
Hours: July 1 to Labor Day, daily from 9:30 a.m. to 5:30 p.m. Labor Day to June 30, daily from 10:00 a.m. to 4:30 p.m.
Admission: Adults $5.50, kids 13-17 $4.00, kids 6-12 $3.00.
Time Allowance: 30 to 90 minutes, depending upon number of houses visited.
Directions (15 miles from Boston): Take I-93 or Rt. 1 and pick up Rt. I-95, then Rt. 114 in Peabody. Drive to the center of Salem and proceed three quarters of the way around the rotary. Take a right onto New Derby Street, go .4 miles to the corner of Hardy Street and you're there.
Parking: Free.
Wheelchair Accessible: No, but video viewing available.
Restaurant: Summer coffee shop.
Picnicking: No.
Rest Rooms: Yes.
Gift Shop: Yes; books and crafts.

SALEM WAX MUSEUM
288 Derby Street
Salem, MA 01970
(508) 740-2WAX

FUN SCALE

Immerse yourself in the sights and sounds of a hundred years of Salem's history. Experience the terror of the witch trials of 1692 and the daring adventures of brave seafarers tackling life on the high seas, all dramatized through realistic wax figures set in niches around a generally dark room.

After being scared to death, walk down to the hands-on activity area. There's a recreation of a fo'c's'le—where a ship's crew sleeps—fully equipped with navy hammocks for swinging in. Then, if you're really feeling nautical, try your hand at knot tying. Other activities allow you to experiment with adding on a Chinese abacus, to put someone on trial and lock them up in a recreated dungeon cell, and to make a gravestone rubbing on a model stone. Or, if you prefer, walk outside to **The Old Burying Point,** the oldest burying ground in Salem. It contains the (genuine!) graves of a Mayflower passenger and a witchcraft trial judge named John Hawthorne. Talk about history!

Age Range: Kids 2-4 no; 5-7 borderline—too scary—but the interactive area downstairs is fun; 8-10 probably; 10 and up yes.

Hours: Sunday through Thursday from 10:00 a.m. to 7:00 p.m., Friday and Saturday from 10:00 a.m. to 10:00 p.m. Off-season (November through March) hours may vary.

Admission: Adults $4.00, seniors $3.50, kids under 14 $2.50.

Time Allowance: 30 to 45 minutes.

Directions (15 miles from Boston): From I 95 (Rt. 128), take Exit 26 (Lowell Street) to Rt. 114 east. Follow signs for downtown Salem and the Visitors Center. The museum is two blocks from the waterfront.

Parking: Meter, free street, and pay-lot.

Wheelchair Accessible: Yes.
Restaurant: No, but nearby.
Picnicking: No.
Rest Rooms: Yes.
Gift Shop: Yes; crystal balls, incense, brooms, knot-tying kits, T-shirts.

SALEM WITCH MUSEUM
Washington Square
Salem, MA 01970
(508) 744-1692

FUN SCALE

What was it like being in Salem in the 1690s? Experience the chilling, multi-sensory presentation at the Salem Witch Museum. The reenacted drama takes place in thirteen life-sized stage settings to eerie sound effects. Witness the startling events that led to the hanging of nineteen innocent victims. It's wicked scary.

Age Range: Kids 2-4 no; 5-7 borderline—too scary; 8 and up, yes.
Hours: Presentations daily every half-hour from 10:00 a.m. to 5:00 p.m.; in July and August, from 10:00 a.m to 7:00 p.m.
Admission: Adults $3.25, children $2.00.
Time Allowance: 30 minutes.
Directions (15 miles from Boston): Take I 93 North (or Rt. 1 North to Rt. I 95 North), then take Rt. 114 East (Exit 25A) in Peabody. Follow signs for "museum information." The museum is across from the Common in the heart of Salem.
Parking: Meter, free street, and pay-lot.
Wheelchair Accessible: Yes.
Restaurant: No, but nearby.
Picnicking: No, but across the street in the park.
Rest Rooms: Yes.
Gift Shop: Yes; pointed hats, scary wrist wrappers, hanging ghost tissue wind socks, T-shirts.

STAGE FORT PARK
Hough Avenue
Gloucester, MA 01930
(508) 281-9790

FUN SCALE

Never underestimate the value of an old tire. At Stage Fort Park, next to Gloucester harbor, is a giant dragon made of recycled tires. Kids love to climb around and through the bumps on its back. In addition to the dragon there is the usual playground paraphernalia: swings, tunnels, slides... Of the two beaches (Cressey and Half Moon), Half Moon is more appealing. To get there you follow the steps carved into the boulders to the crescent-shaped beach below. It's a magical place! There are scads of summer performances under the centrally located gazebo. Kid's stuff too.

Age Range: Any age.
Hours: Dawn to dusk.
Admission: Free
Directions (38 miles from Boston): Take I 95 North to 128 North until the last exit, which will take you to Gloucester. At the "T", take a right. The park is ahead on the left.
Parking: $10.00 per car from Memorial Day to Labor Day.
Restaurant: Snack bar.
cnicking: Yes.
est Rooms: Yes, with showers.

SCHOONER ADVENTURE
Harbor Loop
Gloucester, MA 01931
(508) 281-8079

FUN SCALE

The *Adventure* offers a chance to experience nautical life and catch a bit of history at the same time. Built in 1926, she's a fishing ship with a past. The two-masted, six-sailed wooden vessel is the last Gloucester fishing schooner of its kind.

Having survived the often fierce fishing grounds of the North Atlantic for over eighty years, the *Adventure* is now docked in the harbor until further notice, but her life isn't over yet! Part inn, part museum, part breakfast joint, she offers many possibilities to those who love boats and the sea. Sunday morning breakfast, for instance allows you a chance to see the ship while she's docked and to eat a "cook's choice" breakfast at the same time. Or you might opt for the Bed and Breakfast during the summer, letting the ship rock you to sleep in your cabin and awakening to the smell of fresh-brewed coffee in the morning. Tough life! It is also possible to take a (prearranged) tour, in which you'll learn about

the history of schooners and the growth of the fishing industry. This can be a fun part of a family weekend excursion.

Age Range: Any age, for varying lengths of time.
Hours: Sunday breakfast is offered from October through May from 9:00 a.m. to noon. Bed and Breakfast accommodations are available from Memorial Day through late September, weekends only. Those who wish to take an educational tour should call ahead for time arrangements.
Admission: Sunday breakfast, $5.00 per person. Bed and Breakfast, $45.00-$90.00 per cabin. Tours: Adults $3.00, families $5.00.
Time Allowance: About an hour.
Directions (38 miles from Boston): Take 95 North to 128 North to the last exit, which will take you to Gloucester. At the "T", take a left on Rogers Street. Harbor Loop is ahead on the right and so is the *Adventure*.
Parking: Meter, pay-lot, and some free.
Wheelchair Accessible: No.
Restaurant: Sunday morning breakfast. Menu is cook's choice.
Picnicking: Yes, with prior permission.
Rest Rooms: Yes.
Gift Shop: No.

HAMMOND CASTLE MUSEUM
80 Hesperus Avenue
Gloucester, MA 01930
(508) 283-7673

FUN SCALE

Take a step back in time: Visit a medieval castle. Located on a cliff at the edge of Gloucester harbor, the Hammond Castle is an oddity that is well worth a visit.

It was designed in the late 1920s by an eccentric man named John Hays Hammond. One of America's greatest inventors, Hammond made contributions to radio, TV, and radar technology. He was also a collector, and you will see some of the pieces he brought back from Europe, along with some fascinating inventions.

Elsewhere in the museum you'll experience the deep sounds of the 8,200-pipe organ resonating throughout the Great Hall. It's played at only half volume; imagine the sound at full volume! Hammond was known for his parties, and he must have really rocked out!

The courtyard was Dr. Hammond's favorite area. French medieval pieces are placed alongside Roman ruins, with a swimming pool at the center. The thirty-thousand-gallon pool can be filled with fresh or salt water at the push of a button. The room rains "on command," and there's an artificial moonlight/sunlight system in the roof.

Two bedrooms are open to the public, one gothic, and one early American in style. The gothic bedroom has a floor from a castle in Spain that belonged to

84

Christopher Columbus. The early-American bedroom has disappearing doors. Go inside, close the doors, which are cleverly disguised with wallpaper, and see whether you can find your way out.

Once you do, walk outside and gaze at the building's crazy exterior. Look up at the towers from the Norman period, the gothic flying buttresses, and the French chateau style of the late 1700s. What a combo!

Hammond Castle is not necessarily a place for a four-year-old, but a ten-year-old may enjoy the feeling of being in a medieval castle. The tours are "self-guided," unless previously arranged with the museum.

Age range: Children 2-4 no; 5-7 doubtful, unless they are with someone who can provide entertainment; 8-10 possibly; 10 and up worthwhile.

Hours: Memorial Day to Labor Day, daily from 10:00 a.m. to 5:00 p.m. Winter, Saturday and Sunday from 10:00 a.m. to 5:00 p.m.

Admission: Adults $5.50, seniors and students $4.50, kids (6-12) $3.50.

Time allowance: About an hour.

Directions (38 miles from Boston): Take 128 North to Gloucester(Exit 14). This will put you on 133 East, which you'll follow until the end. Take a right on Rt. 127; one and a half

miles ahead on the left is Hesperus Avenue and the museum.

Parking: Free and ample.
Wheelchair Accessible: No.
Restaurant: No.
Picnicking: Only by permission.
Rest Rooms: Yes.
Gift Shop: Yes; soldiers, postcards, posters.

ANNISQUAM LIGHTHOUSE
45 Norwood Heights
Gloucester, MA 01930
(508) 283-0705

FUN SCALE

A wonderfully New England experience. It's off the beaten track and moderately difficult to find, but once you're there, it's worth it.

Unless you want to look from the outside only, you should call and arrange for David Cornelius, the petty officer, to give you a tour. He'll take you inside and up to the catwalk, which circles around the lighthouse. Check out the windy, scenic coast of Annisquam. Hear a foghorn explanation and all about the duties of a lighthouse keeper. On a foggy day, you may even the foghorn blasting. Block your ears!

Age Range: Any age.
Hours: Private tours spring through fall. Call ahead.
Admission: Free.
Directions (40 miles from Boston): Take Rt. 128 North to the first rotary in Gloucester. Go 3/4 of the way around it and take the exit for Annisquam. Continue for about 3 miles and turn left at the Annisquam Village Church. Take a right 1/2 mile ahead at the sign that says Norwood Heights. Proceed to the end of the road and you're there.
Parking: Free.
Wheelchair Accessible: No.
Restaurant: No.
Picnicking: Yes; choose any rock on the water's edge and crack the picnic basket.
Rest Rooms: No.
Gift Shop: No.

MAUDSLAY STATE PARK
Curzon Mill Road
Newburyport, MA 01950
(508) 465-7223

FUN SCALE

Four hundred fifty acres of wooded, bucolic land are the setting for miles of bikeable, horseback rideable, cross-country skiable, walkable trails. This park is, in a word, spacious. To give you an idea of the park's beauty, its nickname is Rhododendron State Park, because of the multitude of

rhododendrons growing there. It borders the Merrimack River and fishing is allowed.

Bring the insect repellent, though, because at certain times of the year the mosquitoes can be unfriendly. A "Comfort Station" is in the process of being built.

Hours: Dawn to dusk.
Directions (36 miles from Boston): Take I 95 North to the exit for 113 East. Go half a mile and turn left on Noble Street; at the end of road, turn left on Ferry Road. Bear left at the fork and you're there.
Parking: Free and ample.
Restaurant: No.
Picnicking: Yes.
Rest Rooms: No.
Gift Shop: No.

DAVID'S RESTAURANT
The Garrison Inn, On Brown Square, Newburyport, MA 01950
(508) 462-8077

FUN SCALE

At The Garrison Inn in Newburyport is a gourmet restaurant with a good idea. The "Kids Room," run by the staff at David's Restaurant, offers you the option of depositing your children downstairs while you dine in heavenly splendor upstairs. Now why hasn't anyone else thought of that?

It's simple. The "Kid's Room" is open during family dinner hours, from 5:45 p.m. to 8:45 p.m. For a mere $3.15 per child, kids can watch videos, play with other children, and eat from the kiddy menu, which consists of kid-type foods: PBJs, pizza, or fish shapes with chips or fries, and an ice cream cup for dessert. Perfect! This is all done with kind staff supervision. The only rule is that the child be eighteen months or older.

You, meanwhile, treat yourself to the bon-vivant delicacies in either of David's two restaurants. The downstairs restaurant is less expensive and more casual, but still delicious. The upstairs restaurant is truly an elegant experience in epicurean delight.

Rest assured that the kids are well taken care of, and don't forget to collect them on the way out!

Age Range: Eighteen months and up.
Hours: Lunch daily from 11:30 a.m. to 2:00 p.m., Sunday brunch from 9:00 a.m. to 2:00 p.m. Dinner (upstairs restaurant): weekdays from 6:00 to 9:00 p.m., (downstairs restaurant): weekdays from 5:00 to 9:00 p.m., weekends from 5:30 to 10:00 p.m.
The "Kid's Room" is open nightly from 5:45 to 8:45 p.m.; lunch by reservation only.
Admission: "Kid's Room" costs $3.15 per child, including dinner (the child's!).
Time Allowance: As long as it takes to eat a meal.
Directions (36 miles from Boston): Take I 95 North to Exit 57 (Newburyport). Turn right (east) for 2.5 miles and, at the flashing yellow light and the Mall Restaurant, turn left on Green Street. Follow for two blocks and turn left on Pleasant Street. It's one block ahead on the left.
Parking: Free lot behind the Inn.
Wheelchair Accessible: Yes.
Rest Rooms: Yes.
Gift Shop: No.

LE GRAND DAVID
Cabot Street Cinema Theater, 286 Cabot Street
Beverly, MA 01915
(508) 927-3677

FUN SCALE

From the moment you walk through the door, you realize that this will be unlike anything you've ever experienced. A tuxedoed usher greets you, a player piano provides music, and the theater surrounds you with 1920s elegance.

Once the curtain rises, you're mesmerized and swept away by the unfolding of a spectacular performance. From tap dancing and barbershop quartets to classical music and grand stage illusions, such as the old broom suspension trick, the show keeps the audience captivated. The hocus pocusing and abracadabraing are spectacular, performed from start to finish in a handsomely costumed and choreographed style.

It's a family magic show extraordinaire. ¡Vive la magia!

Age Range: 4 years and up.
Hours: Sundays at 3:00 p.m.
Admission: $5.00.
Time Allowance: 2 1/4 hours.
Directions (20 miles from Boston): Take Rt. 1 North to Rt. 128 North until you get to the Beverly exit (22 East). Take Rt. 62 for 2 1/2 miles and, at the intersection, turn right on Cabot Street The theatre is two blocks ahead on the right.
Parking: Municipal parking free on weekends.
Wheelchair Accessible: Yes.
Restaurant: Pastry, cookies, cider.
Picnicking: No.
Rest Rooms: Yes.
Gift Shop: Posters galore and playing card souvenirs.

The **Larcom Theatre,** across from the Beverly City Hall, is run by the same people as the Cabot theatre. In fact, the performers are the same, but it's a different show. They run on Saturdays from October through May, with additional holiday performances. Call for times.

THE WENHAM MUSEUM
132 Main Street,
Wenham, MA 01984
(508) 468-2377

FUN SCALE

The Wenham Museum encompasses an extensive doll collection and the historically preserved Claflin-Richards House, each offering a fun look into the days of old to kids raised in the computer age. The dolls, about a thousand of them, are behind glass—not a hands-on situation, but well worth a peek if you're in the Wenham area. The dolls are of every kind imaginable: china, wood, cloth, paper mache, leather and bisque (a kind of ceramic). Most are antiques from the nineteenth and twentieth centuries. In addition, there are British lead soldiers, doll houses, banks, and teddy bears.

Check out the French Bisque Bébés. Ooh la la! A favorite with kids is the Charles Addams doll house, looming eerily in the center of the room.

The Claflin-Richards House dates from the seventeenth century and offers a pretty good view of life before technology. A large working fireplace is equipped with authentic cooking implements; hanging above are herbs typical of a 1690 herb bed. The other three rooms are from later periods of the house's history: 1690, 1735, and 1850. The rooms are pretty minimal, but what wasn't back then?

Ask your budding social historians how people might have kept warm without central heating. What did they do for fun? Where did they take a bath? The tours are self-guided, but there are plenty of staff members to answers questions.

Age Range: Ages 5 and up, especially doll and soldier enthusiasts.
Hours: Monday through Friday from 11:00 a.m. to 4:00 p.m., Saturday from 1:00 to 4:00 p.m., Sunday from 2:00 to 5:00 p.m. Closed major holidays.
Admission: Adults $3.00, seniors $2.50, children 6 and up $1.00, members free.
Directions (30 miles from Boston): From Rt. 128 North take Exit 20-N and follow Rt. 1A North for 2.3 miles. Museum is on your right before the Wenham Town Hall.
Parking: Free and ample.
Wheelchair Accessible: Yes, on ground level.
Time Allowance: About an hour.
Restaurant: No.
Picnicking: Nearby.
Rest Rooms: Yes.
Gift Shop: Yes; dolls, furniture, sew-it-yourself cloth toys, coloring books.

GOODALE ORCHARDS
133 Argilla Road
Ipswich, MA 01938
(508) 356-5366

FUN SCALE

Anyone up for a FREE hayride? Choose a non-winter day and take a drive out to Goodale Orchard in Ipswich. On Saturdays and Sundays between 11:00 a.m. and 5:00 p.m. the haywagons putter around the farm on a regular basis. Pile on the back and be carted through 150 acres of fields chock full of apples, peaches, tomatoes, zucchini, and blueberries, to name just a few.

Stroll over to the petting zoo area, also known as the barn, and snuggle with a pig or gobble to the turkey.

Leave the food reward until last. It's not difficult to find. Let the glorious aromas of basil, cider donuts, fresh-baked pies, and fruits lead you to the giant barn. Mmmmmmmm!

Events change with the seasons. In the fall, you can expect to see apple pressing demos. November is a big month for pies, and December is Christmas tree time. There's always something happening at Goodale Orchard.

Age Range: There's something for everyone.

Hours: From June to December 23, daily from 9:00 a.m. to 6:00 p.m. Closed December 24 through May, except for May weekends.

Admission: Free.

Time Allowance: 45 to 90 minutes.

Directions (37 miles from Boston): Follow Rt. 1 North to Rt. 128 North. Take Exit 20A (Rt. 1A Hamilton). Ipswich is about ten miles from the exit. Turn right on Rt. 133 East. Follow for about 2 miles and turn right on Northgate Road. Follow the signs.

Parking: Free and plentiful.

Wheelchair Accessible: Yes, but be prepared for bumpy roads and ramps going into the barn.

Restaurant: No, but many baked goods, cider, vegetables, and fruit are for sale.

Picnicking: No picnic tables, but plenty of open space.

Rest Rooms: Yes.

Gift Shop: Fresh vegetables, fruit, wines, cider, T-shirts, baked goods.

ENDICOTT PARK
57 Forest Street
Danvers, MA 01923

FUN SCALE

This 165-acre family park has a lot to offer. **Kidstown** is a large play space equipped with a gazebo, tires, chutes, ladders, wheels, seesaws, and swings. **Lifecourse** is an exercise route for all ages designed to increase strength, flexibility, and endurance. It's set up with paths leading to stations along the way. **The Children's Barnyard** provides a few pettable animals. There's even a pond available for fishing. Dogs are okay, as long as they're on a leash.

Hours: From half an hour before dawn to half an hour after sundown, year round.
Admission: Free.
Directions (18 miles from Boston): Take Rt. 128 North to the exit for Rt. 62. Turn toward Danvers and proceed about one and a half miles. Turn left on Forest Avenue and the park is ahead on the right.
Parking: During the summer, $1.00 per car on weekends and holidays. Free all other times.
Restaurant: No.
Picnicking: Yes.
Rest Rooms: Yes, in the Carriage House.

BREAKHEART RESERVATION
177 Forest Street
Saugus, MA 01906
(617) 233-0834

FUN SCALE

A state-run park full of hikeable, cross-country skiable, jogable trails through 640 acres of hardwood forest punctuated by jagged, rocky outcroppings, two lakes, and a snippet of the Saugus River. Grab your fishing pole and drop your hook into one of the two lakes. Take a dip in the supervised swimming area at Pearce Lake. Go for a hike and birdwatch.

There are oodles of free ranger-conducted programs year-round, suitable for both kids and adults. Some of these include: **Small-Fry Scavenger Hunts, Blueberries for Wee Folk,** and **Fall Foliage Hikes.**

Hours: Dawn to Dusk.
Admission: Free
Directions (12 miles from Boston): Take Rt. 1 North to Lynn Fells Parkway and turn left. Continue on the Parkway one third of a mile, and the reservation is on your right.
Parking: Free and ample.
Picnicking: Yes, with tables and grills.
Rest Rooms: Yes.

ROUTE ONE MINIATURE GOLF
Route 1, Saugus, MA
(617) 233-2811

FUN SCALE

It's the home of the famous giant orange dinosaur! There are also tigers and space ships and all kinds of things scattered about this fifty-year-old golf course. It's easy to see from Route 1, but difficult to reach (see directions). Once you've finally arrived, get in your eighteen holes of miniature golf, play some pinball, or swing at pitches in the batting cage. After you've worked up an appetite, grab a bite to eat from the ice cream stand. It's a kid heaven!

Age Range: 2-4 no; 5-7 possibly; 8 and up yes.
Hours: March through November daily from 10:00 a.m. to 11:00 p.m.
Admission: $3.00 for eighteen holes.
Time Allowance: 30 to 60 minutes.
Directions (5 miles from Boston): Follow Rt. 1 north to Saugus and take the Essex Street exit. It sounds crazy, but cross back *over* Rt. 1 and *reenter*, this time going southbound on Rt. 1. Driving slowly, look ahead for the giant orange dinosaur on the right and, just *before* it, pull off to the right.
Parking: Free.
Wheelchair Accessible: Yes.
Restaurant: Yes; ice cream stand from May through late September.
Picnicking: Yes.
Rest Rooms: Yes.
Gift Shop: No.

WALTER D. STONE ZOO
181 North Street
Stoneham, MA 02180
(617) 438-7459

FUN SCALE

Although the Stone Zoo pales in comparison with other, better-funded zoos, it does have one outstanding feature: the **Aviary**, a sixty-foot-high indoor environment that attempts to replicate the climate of the tropics. With its lush tropical plants and forty species of birds, the Aviary takes you into another world—a hot and humid world of squawks, tweets, hoots, and screeches. You'll feel as if you're in a jungle.

The other animal exhibits are pretty minimal: a polar bear, some flamingos, a few monkeys. There is a five-year plan for major renovations and additions, however, so don't rule the zoo out. It also has a free playground full of fun equipment right outside the gates.

Age Range: Any age.
Hours: Daily from 10:00 a.m. to 4:00 p.m.
Admission: Adults (12 and up) $2.00; kids (4-12), seniors, students, and uniformed military $1.00.
Time Allowance: About an hour.
Directions (10 miles from Boston): Take I 93 North to Exit 36. Turn right at the first light and the zoo is on the right.
Parking: Free and ample.
Wheelchair Accessible: Yes.
Restaurant: Yes, a snack bar. (Stay away from the pizza!)
Picnicking: Yes.
Rest Rooms: Yes.
Gift Shop: Yes, T-shirts, tote bags, bumper stickers.

DANFORTH MUSEUM OF ART

Framingham, MA 01701
(508) 620-0050

FUN SCALE

Although small in size, The Danforth Museum of Art has a lot to offer. In addition to its extensive permanent collection focusing on eighteenth-to-twentieth-century American art, there are special exhibits of works on loan from artists, museums, and private collections.

Activity booklets are available for kids to help them gain an understanding of and interest in the art. Answer the thought-provoking and challenging questions while viewing fantastic masterpieces.

The Ballou Junior Gallery is a place for kids (with parent supervision) to explore scientific phenomena that tie art together with the gallery's current theme, whatever it is. Hands-on activities complement the exhibit and enrich the child's appreciation of art and the world around them.

Age Appropriate: Kids 2-4 no; 5-7 will enjoy the Ballou Junior Gallery; 8 and up yes.
Hours: Wednesday through Sunday from 12:00 noon to 5:00 p.m.
Admission: Adults $3.00, students and seniors $2.00, members and children under 12 free.
Time Allowance: 1 hour.
Directions (25 miles from Boston): Take the Mass Pike (Rt. 90) to Exit 13. Follow Rt. 126 to Union Avenue. Turn right and go about a quarter mile; the museum will be on the right.
Parking: Free and available.
Wheelchair Accessible: Yes.
Restaurant: No, but nearby.
Picnicking: Yes, on lawn in front.
Gift Shop: Yes; cool T-shirts, mask kits, Escher ties, flint arrowheads.

DECORDOVA MUSEUM AND SCULPTURE PARK
51 Sandy Pond Road, Lincoln, MA 01773
(617) 259-8355

FUN SCALE

The Decordova Museum introduces people to important trends in contemporary art, especially in the works of New England artists. Works of art from painting to sculpture, from conceptualism to realism, are strongly displayed in and around the thirty-five acres of museum property. Over forty outdoor works grace DeCordova's sculpture park, the only one of its kind in New England. The sculptures vary in media, size, color, and purpose. They're large, for the most part, and are available for many degrees of interaction. Picnicking alongside one of the awesome sculptures is allowed and even encouraged.

Age Range: Ages 2-7 can have fun playing in sculpture garden; 8 and up yes.
Hours: Tuesday through Friday from 10:00 a.m. to 5:00 p.m.; weekends from 12:00 noon to 5:00 p.m. The sculpture park is open daily from 8:00 a.m. to 10:00 p.m.
Admission: Adults $4.00; seniors, students, and children (6 and up) $3.00. The sculpture park is free.
Time Allowance: 45 minutes to 2 hours (with picnicking).
Directions (12 miles from Boston): Take the Mass Pike (I 90) to 128 North to Exit 28B. Follow it west for three miles until you come to an intersection. Go straight through to Sandy Pond Road. The museum is a half a mile ahead on the right.
Parking: Free and ample.
Wheelchair Accessible: Partially.
Restaurant: No.
Picnicking: Yes.
Rest Rooms: Yes.
Gift Shop: No.

97

DRUMLIN FARM NATURE CENTER AND WILDLIFE SANCTUARY
South Great Road, Lincoln, MA 01773
(617) 259-9807

FUN SCALE

Pigs, mules, chickens, eagles, radishes, woodchucks, rabbits, foxes, okra, Belgian draft horses, lambs, string beans, human beings...

Though owned and run by The Massachusetts Audubon Society, Drumlin Farm isn't a "birds only" situation. It's a place where farm animals and gardens thrive in Eden-like luxuriance. **The Food Project** encourages respect for the land and develops wisdom about growing and harvesting skills. Check out the spectacular landscape, from the **Butterfly Garden** near the entrance to the pastoral setting of the back field.

Go to the **Burrowing Animal Building** and see the woodchuck, fox, rabbit, and possum. Do you smell a skunk? Most likely it's the fox. They have scent glands in their feet for marking territory. If you can't find any of the burrowers outside, go inside to the dark underground space where you can look at the critters through glass. Oh, spooky!

All of the animals at the sanctuary were brought in hurt and are in captivity for their own protection.

For some hands-on action, go to the **Skull Room**. Can you guess whose skull is whose? In the **Tack Room** you'll learn how to groom a horse. Do you know how to tell a pony from a horse? A pony is only fourteen hands plus two inches from the withers down.

Climb up on the big old red tractor and pretend you're Farmer Brown. Check to see whether one of the sows has a litter of piglets. And don't forget to look in on the chickens in the **Poultry House**—I'll bet you didn't know there were so many different kinds! There really is a pecking order. Dominant birds peck out the feathers of the weaker hens, especially in the winter. That's why some are barebacked. The feathers do grow back in, though.

The Hayride is an ongoing event and shouldn't be missed. For $1.00 you'll go bumpity-bumping around the grounds in a haycart hauled by a tractor. Fun!

There are many scheduled events. Call for information.

Age Appropriate: 2 and up. There are zillions of pettable animals and activities to be awed by.
Hours: April to November, Tuesday through Sunday from 9:00 a.m. to 5:00 p.m.; closed Mondays except holidays. November 1 to March 31, Tuesday through Sunday from 9:00 a.m. to 4:00 p.m.; closed Mondays except holidays.
Admission: Adults $5.00, children (3-15) and seniors $3.50.
Time Allowance: 1-3 hours.
Directions (12 miles from Boston): Take Interstate 90 West to Rt. 128 North. Take a left on Rt. 117 and it's on the left (about 5 miles) before you get to Lincoln.
Parking: Free and plentiful.
Handicap Accessible: Yes, in that there are no steps. There's one long, steep hill, however.
Restaurant: No.
Picnicking: Yes.
Gift Shop: Yes; books, binoculars, jewelry, and ceramics.

WORCESTER ART MUSEUM
55 Salisbury Street
Worcester, MA 01609
(508) 799-4406

FUN SCALE

Regarded as a "jewel" among art museums, The Worcester Art Museum is well worth a visit. The building houses more than thirty thousand pieces spanning fifty centuries of Eastern and Western cultures. The thirty-five galleries offer visitors a walk through time and across cultures.

Begin your exploration with the art of ancient Egypt, Greece, and Rome.

Continue through the many other galleries of art from the Middle Ages (including a twelfth-century Romanesque chapter house); the Asian collection of prints, textiles, sculpture, and paintings; European masterpieces from the thirteenth through the twentieth centuries; an impressive Meso-

American gallery with art from 1200 to 300 BC; and the museum's outstanding contemporary collection.

The museum was one of the first to exhibit and collect photographs as fine art. Kudos! The collection is extensive, encompassing work by such greats as Steiglitz, Weston, and Cartier-Bresson, and they're displayed in changing exhibitions.

The museum also offers a **Discovery Room** where kids can try their hand at techniques used by artists. There are summer art programs for kids too.

Age Range: Kids 2-4 no; 5-7 possibly, with the right parents as guides, 8 and up yes.
Hours: Tuesday through Friday from 11:00 a.m. to 4:00 p.m., Saturday from 10:00 a.m. to 5:00 p.m., and Sunday from 1:00 to 5:00 p.m. Closed Mondays and major holidays.
Admission: Adults $5.00; Groups of 10 or more $4.50; seniors, students with college ID, and youths (13-18) $3.00; kids 12 and under free; free for all on Saturdays from 10:00 a.m. to 12:00 noon.
Time Allowance: 1-3 hours.
Directions (42 miles from Boston): Take the Massachusetts turnpike to Exit 10 (Auburn) and get on I 290 East. Take Exit 17 and turn left on Rt. 9. Go through 3 sets of lights and turn right on Harvard Street. The museum is ahead on the left.
Parking: Free.
Wheelchair Accessible: Yes.
Restaurant: Cafe open Tuesday to Saturday 11:30 a.m. to 2:00 p.m.
Picnicking: In courtyard by permission.
Rest Rooms: Yes.
Gift Shop: Yes; Jewlry, poster, T-shirts.

HIGGINS ARMORY
100 Barber Avenue
Worcester, MA 01606
(508) 853-6015

FUN SCALE

If you're an armory buff, then this is the place for you. Bordering Worcester, and rather difficult to find (see directions), the Higgins Armory is a glass and steel building constructed in 1931 by a slightly eccentric man named John Woodman Higgins.

Higgins, born in 1874, had long been enchanted by tales of knights and knighthood, a fascination that led him to a life-long interest in steel and armories. Over the years he gained an extensive collection of armor, and in 1931 his dream of housing it in a steel museum came true.

The tour begins in a comfortable auditorium with a video on the curious history of the Higgins Armory. The building alone is something to see. Inspired by the castles and noble houses Higgins visited in his travels, it features a gothically influenced **Great Hall** where knights in shining armor pose motionless astride life-sized horses.

The fourth-floor exhibits are arranged chronologically, from ancient armor to modern. From an example of natural armor (the back of an armadillo) to a synthetic motorcycle helmet, you'll travel through the history of armor.

The second floor houses **The Quest Gallery,** an assortment of interactive activities. If you've always wanted to look like Sir Lancelot or Lady Guenevere, now's your chance. Try on some of the castle clothing and helmets available in the gallery. Build a fort with Leggos, design your own coat of arms, and make a brass rubbing to take home.

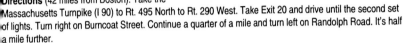

Age Range: 5 and up.

Hours: Tuesday through Saturday from 10:00 a.m. to 4:00 p.m., Sunday from 12:00 noon to 4:00 p.m. Open Mondays in July and August, 10:00 a.m. to 4:00 p.m.

Admission: Adults $4.75, seniors $4.00, kids(6-16) $3.75.

Time Allowance: 1 to 3 hours.

Directions (42 miles from Boston): Take the Massachusetts Turnpike (I 90) to Rt. 495 North to Rt. 290 West. Take Exit 20 and drive until the second set of lights. Turn right on Burncoat Street. Continue a quarter of a mile and turn left on Randolph Road. It's half a mile further.

Parking: Free and ample.

Wheelchair Accessible: Yes.

Restaurant: No, just vending machines for snacks.

Picnicking: Yes, open space across the street.

Rest Rooms: Yes.

Gift Shop: Yes; T-shirts, soldiers, posters, stamps.

NEW ENGLAND SCIENCE CENTER
222 Harrington Way
Worcester, MA 01604
(508) 791-9211

FUN SCALE

Take some time to discover the world of science. Plan to spend several hours, because there's a lot to explore! The New England Science Center is definitely a "kid friendly" environment and worthwhile for any age.

Inside the museum are three floors of interactive exhibits designed to stimulate and challenge. The focus is on the environment. Dynamic programs throughout provide you with an understanding of the environmental consequences of human actions and offer solutions for problems threatening Planet Earth.

There's plenty to do. Listen to the myriad ways animals communicate in the **Infospheres** exhibit. Touch computer screens to find out the latest information about computers and human behavior. Dive under the sea in the **Dynamics of the Depths** exhibit: Explore some of the creatures up close in the touch tank and view others through glass. Under the same roof are the Alden Omnisphere and Norton Observatory; each takes you on incredible journeys to "worlds beyond." Kids love operating the miniature robot in the **Robotics** exhibit. Other interactive computers supplement many of the exhibits, providing fun while illuminating issues of science and the pressing environmental concerns of today. And, speaking of environmental concerns, be sure and check out the

Abiding Locally, Thinking Globally exhibit. It reflects the Science Center's philosophy, the need for greater global awareness of present-day concerns.

Sixty acres of natural wonders surround the museum. Experience the **Live Wildlife Center** and see mountain lions, polar bears diving in and out of the water, a non-soaring Bald Eagle, and frogs. Did you know that frogs don't drink water? They absorb moisture through their skin.

Look through the telescope in the unit that looks like a silver silo and see the solar system up close. A fifteen-minute ride on the **Explorer Train** is optional for 1.00; the train circles the entire New England Science Center and is a definite hit with the younger set.

Age Range: There's something for everyone.

Hours: Monday through Saturday from 10:00 a.m. to 5:00 p.m., Sundays from 12:00 noon to 5:00 p.m.

Admission: Adults $6.00; kids (3-16), seniors, and students $4.00.

Time Allowance: 2 to 4 hours.

Directions (42 miles from Boston): Traveling east on I-90, take Exit 10 to 290 East. From here, take Exit 14 and turn left onto Grafton Street. At the second traffic light, turn right onto Franklin Street, go through the first set of lights, and take your second right onto Harrington Way.

Parking: Free and plentiful.

Wheelchair Accessible: Yes.

Restaurant: Yes, The Hungry Bear Snack shop.

Picnicking: Yes.

Rest Rooms: Yes.

Gift Shop: Yes; T-shirts, place mats, dinosaur models and games, posters, and books.

OLD STURBRIDGE VILLAGE
1 Old Sturbridge Village Road
Sturbridge, MA 01566
(508) 347-3362

FUN SCALE

For a taste of life from the late eighteenth to the early nineteenth century, spend the day at Old Sturbridge Village. Costumed staff believably demonstrate work in the gardens, homes, and farms. In fact, they take on the roles so realistically, you might forget that it's the twentieth century and you're only visiting.

Begin the tour with the orientation slide show in the theater. It's fifteen minutes of nineteenth-century family life told with an old man's voice looking through a boy's eyes. Watch and listen as he recounts how he broke his sister's doll, and what happened

afterward. There are scenes of typical farm life in old New England.

Events take place throughout the day on a regular basis. If a talk on nineteenth-century beekeeping is

of interest, head over to the cidermill. **The Fitch House** is the site for ironing demonstrations, while the **Fenno Barn** and the **Brick Theater** feature storytelling presentations.

Kids will love climbing on the horse-drawn wagon and traveling around the grounds. Any gardeners in your family? Take a walk through the herb garden and note the informatively labeled herbs. They're color-coded for culinary, household, and medicinal use. Stop and watch the woman quilting those intricately designed patches.

There's a lot to do and a lot to see. Plan to spend several hours.

Age Range: Kids 2-4 probably not; 5-7 might enjoy walking around and seeing the costumes and animals; 8 and up yes, but teenagers might not think it's cool enough.

Hours: From November 1 April 1 Tuesday through Sunday from 10:00 a.m. to 4:00 p.m. From April 2 to October 30, daily from 9:00 a.m. to 5:00 p.m.

Admission: Adults $15.00, kids (6-15) $7.50. Second-consecutive-day visit free with ticket validation.

Time Allowance: 2-3 hours.

Directions (58 miles from Boston): Take the Massachusetts Turnpike (I-90) to Exit 9; follow signs, taking care not to miss the Sturbridge Village sign on the left.

Parking: Free and ample.

Wheelchair Accessible: Yes, most exhibits.

Restaurant: Buffet Room open from 11:00 a.m. to 2:30 p.m.; cafeteria open from 9:30 a.m. to 4:00 p.m.

Picnicking: Yes.

Rest Rooms: Yes.

Gift Shop: Yes; candles, postcards, T-shirts.

THE BUTTERFLY PLACE AT PAPILLON PARK
120 Tyngsborough Road
Westford, MA 01886
(508) 392-0955

FUN SCALE

Just when you thought that life couldn't get any more unbelievable, along comes a butterfly museum located in the middle of a field in Westford. Butterflys, moths, caterpillars, and more butterflys are housed in a 3,100-square-foot glass atrium filled with magnificent flora.

Start your experience with an informational video, then check out the glass displays of different metamorphic stages of the Lepidoptera (butterfly and moth order).

Move inside the atrium and watch the creatures flutter about freely, dancing from flower to flower. They need heat to fly actively, and if you catch them in the morning, you'll see them, wings outstretched, basking in the sun. They do this to energize for a full day of butterfly activity.

The time of year determines what you'll see. Silk moths, for instance, are active in the spring, while late summer and fall are monarch season. No fools, the monarchs from New England migrate to Mexico come cold weather. If you're lucky, you'll see a Cecropia caterpillar with bright orange and yellow tubercles on a lime-green body. These ball-like projections are used for protection and energy storage. It's mind-blowing to think that such a brilliantly colored creature could metamorphosize into a moth.

The life span of a butterfly ranges from one week to six months. No wonder the exhibit is always evolving! It's a butterfly lover's trip to paradise.

Age Range: Any age. Second grade is ideal.
Hours: April 15 through Halloween, daily from 10:00 a.m. to 5:00 p.m.
Admission: Adults $6.00, seniors and children (3-12) $5.00.
Time Allowance: About an hour.
Directions (36 miles from Boston): Take the Massachusetts Turnpike (I 90) West to the exit for Rt. 128 North. Follow 128 North to Rt. 3 North. Take Exit 34 to Westford Road toward Westford, bearing left onto Swan Road, which becomes Tyngsboro Road. The park is on the right about a mile from Exit 34.
Parking: Free and ample.
Wheelchair Accessible: Yes.
Restaurant: No.
Picnicking: Yes.
Rest Rooms: Yes.
Gift Shop: Yes; papillon hatching kits, books, cards.

GREAT BROOK FARM STATE PARK
841 Lowell Street
Carlisle, MA 01741
(508) 369-6312

FUN SCALE

Forget your cholesterol hang-ups and head for the ice cream stand at Great Brook State Farm. Okay, eating the creamy ice cream isn't mandatory, but it certainly is tempting.

Visit and observe firsthand the modern New England dairy farm. Ramble around the twenty acres of trails on your own, or join one of the scheduled tours offered by the Park Interpreter. Tour times are posted in the exhibit area of the barn.

ander around and look at the ducks in the pond, the goats and sheep in the pasture, d, of course, the cows.

There's a lot to learn about these wonderful creatures. To begin with, they eat a enomenal amount. The common bovine consumes approximately fifteen pounds of ain and eighty pounds of fermented hay and washes it down with about thirty gallons water a day. Appreciate that ice cream cone!

Evening milkings take place at 6:30. Slurp your cones while watching the cows ing milked on the other side of the huge picture window.

e Range: All ages.
urs: The ice cream stand is open mid-ril through Halloween from 11:00 a.m. dusk.
mission: Free.
e Allowance: Varies, depending on l-walking interest.
ections (22 miles from Boston): Take 128 North to Rt. 225 West to Carlisle nter. Turn right on Lowell Street. It's miles ahead on the right.
rking: Free and plentiful.
eelchair Accessible: Yes, for the st part.
staurant: Ice cream stand.
nicking: Yes.
st Rooms: Yes.

109

THE DISCOVERY MUSEUMS
177 Main Street
Acton, MA 01720
(508) 264-4200

FUN SCALE

"Imagination is more important than knowledge." These words of Albert Einstein greet you at the entrance to the museum, summing up the philosophy of its directors. At the Discovery Museums, the atmosphere is one of discovery,

imagination, and creativity.

The CHILDREN'S DISCOVERY MUSEUM is located in a beautiful old Victorian house converted into a series of theme rooms. It's a hands-on experimenting museum with a learn-through-play philosophy.

Step back a few hundred million years in time and go into the **Dinosaur Room.** Play with the huge dino wall puzzle and stuffed animals; check out a fossil.

Moving right along to the topic of water...Aside from being a life-staple, water is the basis for some pretty cool phenomena. Experiment with the "bubble hoop" and surround yourself with a giant bubble. Awesome!

Like beaches? The museum keeps one in a closet—a peaceful space fitted out with the sights, sounds, and textures of a beach. Or, for you tree lovers, pretend you're in a forest in the **Woodland Room.** Climb a tree. Listen to the surrounding animal calls. Crawl through a tunnel into the world of burrowing animals.

Dress up in a lion costume, climb the tree house, and embark on a wild adventure in the **Safari Room**; create your own rainbow with the "Rainbow Spinner" in the **Rainbow Room.** Then return to New England and climb aboard the **Discovery Ship** in the model maritime setting. Kids love it.

THE SCIENCE

DISCOVERY MUSEUM, located behind The Children's Discovery Museum, is designed especially for bigger kids (ages 6 and up) and focuses on science savviness using discovery and exploration skills. Yes, it's smaller than its Boston counterpart, The Museum of Science (also known as "Papa Bear"), but it's comprehensible and fun.

Before even entering the museum, grab a partner and try out the **Whisper Dishes.** As your partner listens at one parabolic dish, speak softly into the other and prepare to be amazed as the sound is transmitted to your partner a hundred feet away!

Climb up to the **Tower Court,** a cupola space used for scientific explorations, including a giant Mist Tornado, elongated Listening Tubes, Ninja Balls, and an incredible Air Harp. Go into the **Air Harp Room,** wrapped around with a mural of blue sky and white puffy clouds, and notice the beams of red light shooting from the ceiling to the floor. Where's the Air Harp? Each beam of light is equivalent to a harp string. Move your arm through the strings of light and listen. Conduct your own orchestra. Breathtaking!

Invent something in the **Inventor's Workshop.** Take something apart at the take-apart table, put it together again, and take it home.

Explore concepts in math and topography on wall-sized geoboards, puzzles, and a math mirror. Create a wild spirographic pattern with a laser. Use the **Swinging Science Harmonograph Table** to create something to take home. Choose a color, lock the table, stand back, and watch. *Voilà*: a colorful, elliptically curved pattern appears before your eyes. Roll it up and take it home.

Age Range: Children's Discovery Museum, toddler to age 9; Science Discovery Museum, 6 and up, with overlapping in each.

Hours: Tuesday, Thursday, and Friday from 1:00 to 4:30 p.m.; Wednesday from 1:00 to 6:00 p.m. (Science Museum only) and from 9:00 a.m. to 4:30 p.m.

(Children's Museum only); Saturday and Sunday from 9:00 a.m. to 4:30 p.m.

Summer Hours (both museums): Tuesday through Sunday from 9:00 a.m. to 4:30 p.m., Wednesday from 9:00 a.m. to 7:00 p.m. Closed Monday.

Admission: $5.00 per person for each museum; $8.00 for both museums on the same day.

Time Allowance: 1-3 hours.

Directions (23 miles from Boston): Take Rt. 2 West, then Rt. 27 South toward Maynard (not Acton). One mile down Rt. 27 are the museums on the left. Look for the giant green dinosaur out front.

Parking: Free and plentiful.

Wheelchair Accessible: Yes.

Restaurant: No, but close by.

Picnicking: Yes, uncovered.

Rest Rooms: Yes.

Gift Shop: Yes; small museum items—pencils, T-shirts.

HULL LIFESAVING MUSEUM
1117 Nantasket Avenue
Hull, MA 02045
(617) 925-LIFE

FUN SCALE

Don't let the fact that it's next to the sewage treatment plant, or that it's unassuming from the outside, mislead you. The Hull Lifesaving Museum, and I'm not talking about the candy with the hole in the middle, is full of hands-on educational activities, and well worth a stop.

Learn about rescues at sea in a U.S. Life Saving Station that was founded back in 1889. Boston harbor, with its many shallow spots, busy ocean traffic, and strong storms, is a particularly likely spot for a lifesaving station. The lifesavers went out in the middle of storms armed with surf boats and breeches buoys. Go ahead: Try on a pair of breeches attached to a buoy and see what it's like.

Learn about the everyday life of the surfmen (lifesavers) by looking at their galle (kitchen), messroom (dining room), and bunk room (sleeping quarters). See the surf boat *Nantasket* in the boat room. Try your hand at knot tying. Tap on the telegraph keys and send a message in Morse code. Go up to the attic and learn about navigation, while playing with costumes and boats. Climb up to the cupola, look through the binoculars, and imagine finding ships in distress. Ready for the rescue?

Age Range: Kids 2-4 possibly; 5 and up yes.
Hours: July 1 through Labor Day, Wednesday through Saturday from 12:00 noon to 5:00 p.m.; the rest of year, Saturday and Sunday and Monday holidays from 12:00 noon to 5:00 p.m. Open any time by appointmen
Admission: Adults $3.00, seniors $2.00, kids (5-17) $1.50.
Directions (16 miles from Boston): Take Rt. 93 South Rt. 3 South. Get off at Exit 14 and follow Rt. 228 out to Nantasket. Following the small buoy-shaped museum signs go about 3 miles, almost to the end of the peninsula. The museum is next to the sewage treatme plant. If you're truly lost, follow your nose.
Parking: Free.
Wheelchair Accessible: Yes, first floor only.
Restaurant: No, but nearby.
Picnicking: Yes, on seawall across street.
Rest Rooms: Yes.
Gift shop: Yes; ocean-theme T-shirts, placemats and great books.

CAROUSEL UNDER THE CLOCK
205 Nantasket Avenue
Nantasket Beach, Hull, MA 02045
(617) 925-0472

FUN SCALE

One of about 150 antique wooden carousels still operating in the United States today, the Carousel under the Clock is located next to Nantasket beach. Sixty-six horses, forty-two of which are jumpers, and two Roman chariots rotate to tunes provided by a Wurlitzer 153-band organ.

Age Range: Any age.
Hours: Late March through late May and during the month of October, weekends from 9:00 a.m. to 10:00 p.m. June through September, daily from 9:00 a.m. to 10:00 p.m.
Admission: $1.50 per ride and $7.00 for 6 rides.
Time Allowance: 5 minutes per ride.
Directions (15 miles from Boston): Take Rt. 93 South to Rt. 3 South. Get off at Exit 14 and follow Rt. 228 to Nantasket. You'll see the carousel on the left of the major boardwalk.
Parking: Free or pay lots and street parking.
Wheelchair Accessible: Yes.
Restaurant: No.
Picnicking: Yes.
Rest Rooms: Yes.

ART COMPLEX MUSEUM
189 Alden Street
Duxbury, MA 02331
(617) 934-6634

FUN SCALE

Whether you're interested in the art inside or nature's art outside, you might enjoy a visit to the Art Complex Museum in Duxbury. Contemporary architecture in a meditative setting sets the stage for rotating exhibits ranging from works of contemporary New England artists in traveling shows to pieces from the Museum's permanent collection. The museum is particularly known for its Shaker furniture, Asian art, and American paintings.

Summer Sundays at 2:00 p.m., you can learn about the Japanese tea ceremony. The tea ceremony presentation take place in a tea hut situated in a Japanese garden on the museum grounds.

There are also art classes for kids, from preschoolers through middle-schoolers. Call for schedules.

Age Range: 2 and up yes, for the kids' programs, but the museum offers nothing hands-on.
Hours: Wednesday through Sunday from 1:00 to 4:00 p.m.
Admission: Free.
Time Allowance: 30 to 60 minutes.
**Directions (50 miles from

Boston):** Take Rt. 3 South to Exit 11. Turn right on 14 East and proceed two miles to first traffic light at 3A. Turn right, and Alden Street will be your first left.
Parking: Free and plentiful.
Wheelchair Accessible: Yes.
Restaurant: No.
Picnicking: Yes, next to the pond.
Rest Rooms: Yes.
Gift Shop: No; but postcards available.

PLYMOUTH ROCK
Plymouth Harbor
Plymouth, MA 02362

FUN SCALE

Free and always "open" (How can a rock be closed?) to the public is the fantastically famous Plymouth Rock. Sitting, rock-like, next to the harbor, it stands ready for the next awestruck tourist to breathe those timeless words: "You mean that's it?" Granted, it's probably less extraordinary than expected, but it *is* an important "chunk" of our history. You might use the Plymouth Rock as the starting point of your Plymouth adventure.

Directions: (55 miles from Boston): Take Exit 6 from Rt. 3 South and turn right. Cross Rt. 3A and, at the rotary, bear to the right. It's ahead on the left. You can't miss it. Then again maybe you can!
Parking: Meter and lot parking.
Time: 30 seconds to 5 minutes.

CRANBERRY WORLD
Ocean Spray Cranberries, Inc.
Water Street, Plymouth, MA 02360
(508) 747-2350

FUN SCALE

Ocean Spray Cranberries Inc. has created a top-notch informational visitor's center located on the edge of the Plymouth harbor. Learn about the fascinating world of the cranberry. One of the only fruits native to this country (two others are blueberries and Concord grapes), the bitter little berry has quite a history.

Ever tried to bounce a cranberry? The quality control bounce machine does it all day. Ask to see a demo on how the cranberry is rated for its bounceability. The higher bouncers go into fresh fruit bags, while the lower bouncers go into the juices. The non-bouncers go out to western Massachusetts to a gigantic compost pile. (By the way, inner air pockets are responsible for their bounce.)

Check out the five-minute video on how cranberries are grown. You take a common peat swamp, add some cranberry vines, cover the bog with water each winter (for protection), wait for three to five years for the vines to bear fruit, and then, come September, harvest away.

Pick up the phone at the diorama for other cranberry tidbits. Later, downstairs, you can sample some of the many varieties of cranberry juices. If you're lucky, you can catch a cooking demo (samples served afterward!).

Rumor has it that if all the cranberries that were harvested last year by Ocean Spray were strung together, they would circle the globe forty times. Has anyone tried this?

Massachusetts is the largest producer of cranberries in the USA. Hooray!

Don't forget to check out October's **Cranberry Harvest Festival** in Carver, Massachusetts. It's free, and provides a chance to see the harvesting machines in action. Call Cranberry World for specifics.

Age Range: Kids 2-7 won't be too interested, but they will enjoy the free juice and goodies at the end. Kids 8 and up, yes.

Hours: From May 1 to November 30, daily from 9:30 a.m. to 5:00 p.m.

Admission: Free.

Time Allowance: 20 to 30 minutes.

Directions (55 miles from Boston): Take Exit 6 from Rt. 3 South and turn right. Cross Rt. 3A toward the water and circle 3/4 around the rotary to Water Street. It's 1/3 mile ahead on the right.

Parking: Free and plentiful.

Wheelchair Accessible: Yes.

Restaurant: No.

Picnicking: No.

Rest rooms: Yes.

Gift Shop: Yes.

PLIMOTH PLANTATION
137 Warren Avenue
Plymouth, MA 02360
(508) 746-1622

FUN SCALE

Leave the twentieth century behind. Step back to 1627 and become part of a living history experience at Plimoth Plantation.

Through its various exhibits, Plimoth Plantation seeks to recreate the people, time, and place of seventeenth-century Plymouth. With their mannerisms, dress, and speech, specially trained staff—men, women, and children— play the parts of real historical people from the first Pilgrim settlement. Get into the spirit of the 1620s and

strike up a conversation with one of the Pilgrims. Find out what it was like to come here and build a future, as your informant speaks in one of the seventeen dialects heard throughout the village. You'll get to know them as people, not the stern subjects so often depicted in textbooks, as you watch them go about their daily tasks—cooking, harvesting, and tending the farm

animals. You might even offer to lend a hand.

An equally important part of the story involves the Native Americans. Walk over to **Hobbamock's Homesite** and look at a seventeenth-century Wampanoag dwelling. Contemporary Native Americans, some dressed in seventeenth-century Wampanoag clothing and others in street clothes, will show you around and answer questions. You'll see bark-covered wetus (houses) and assorted artifacts of daily life from that time. It's illuminating to see the Native American and Pilgrim cultures side by side.

Peace between the Pilgrims and the Wampanoags held for more than half a century before the expanding English population brought tension and fighting. Feel free to chat with the Wampanoag staff. They're willing to talk about the past as well as the present Native American situation.

Age range: Kids 2-4 doubtful; 5 and up yes.
Hours: April 1 through December 5, daily from 9:00 a.m. to 5:00 p.m.
Admission: Adults $15.00, kids(6-12) $11.00. Plimoth Plantation/Mayflower II Combo prices: Adults $18.50, kids (6-12) $11.00.
Time Allowance: Up to four hours.
Directions (55 miles from Boston): Take I93 South to Rt. 3 South. Take Exit 4 in Plymouth and follow the signs.
Parking: Free and plentiful.
Wheelchair Accessible: Visitor's and Craft Centers, yes; Village no, but there's a video viewing room for those unable to make the trip down to the village.
Restaurant: Yes.
Picnicking: Yes.
Rest Rooms: Yes.
Gift Shop: Yes; tea towels, Pilgrim hats, blown glass items, mugs, videos.

MAYFLOWER II
State Pier
Plymouth Harbor, MA 02362
(508) 746-1622

FUN SCALE

The *Mayflower's* great—a full-scale replica of the ship that brought Pilgrims to the New World back in the fall of 1620, anchored right in Plymouth Harbor. Come up the gangway and board the ship, where trained Plimoth Plantation staff members realistically act out the roles of grimy boat people who have been at sea for months on end searching for religious freedom. Ask them about their long journey and about life during the seventeenth century. Can you and the kids imagine taking a long sea voyage on the *Mayflower* with 101 other people? Incidentally, many of those on board were not even Pilgrims. How do you suppose they all got along? (And you thought long car rides were difficult!)

Age Range: Kids 2-4 possibly, at the upper end of the scale; 5 and up yes.

Hours: April 1 through December 5, daily from 9:00 a.m. to 5:00 p.m.

Admission: Adults $5.75, kids (6-12) $3.75. See combo price listed under Plimoth Plantation.

Time Allowance: 30 minutes.

Directions (55 miles from Boston): Take Exit 6 from Rt. 3 South and turn right. Cross Rt. 3A and, at the rotary, bear to the right. It's ahead on the left. You can't miss it.

Parking: Meter and paylot.

Wheelchair Accessible: No.

Restaurant: No, but nearby.

Picnicking: Yes, nearby.

Rest Rooms: Yes, nearby.

Gift Shop: Yes; tea towels, candles, baked goods.

PLYMOUTH NATIONAL WAX MUSEUM
16 Carver Street
Plymouth, MA 02360
(508) 746-6468

FUN SCALE

The site is Cole's Hill in Plymouth, where the Pilgrims were secretly buried during their first rugged winter—secretly, so that the Indians wouldn't find out how many Pilgrims had died. The Wax Museum, overlooking Plymouth Rock and Plymouth Harbor, is an appropriate site for a museum that relives the Pilgrim story through a 3-D wax (really plastic) show.

The twenty-six-scene exhibit begins with a meeting in Scrooby, England, where the Pilgrims, formerly Separatists, decide to escape England's religious restrictions and leave for Holland. After a series of mishaps, the Pilgrims arrive in their new homeland. Find out what leads up to their landing in Plymouth. It's all done to special sound and lighting effects. (Flashlights are available for scaredy cats.) This is a great visual way for your kids and you to learn how it all began back in 1606.

Age Range: Kids 2-4 probably not; 5 and up yes.
Hours: Spring through fall daily from 9:00 a.m. to 5:00 p.m.
Admission: Adults $5.00, children (5-12) $2.00, Under 5 free.
Time allowance: 1/2 hour.

Directions (55 miles from Boston): Take Rt. I-93 South to Rt. 3 South, to Rt. 44 (Exit 6). At end of ramp, turn right on Rt. 44. At traffic light turn right on to Rt. 3A. Take the sixth left on North Street. At the fork in the road, bear right.
Parking: Meter or pay-lot.
Wheelchair Accessible: No.
Restaurant: No, but nearby.
Picnicking: No, but nearby.
Rest rooms: Yes.
Gift shop: Yes; calendars, mugs, candles.

PILGRIM HALL MUSEUM
75 Court Street (Rt. 3A)
Plymouth, MA 02360
(508) 746-1620

FUN SCALE

Built in 1824, Pilgrim Hall was America's first public museum. Although small in size, it has some pretty cool things on display, from Native American artifacts, to a model of the *Mayflower,* to a fragment of Plymouth Rock. (Plymouth Rock was once four or five times its present size, and no wonder.)

This museum contains *original* Pilgrim artifacts, now 370-odd years old. Ask for the **Treasure Hunt Guide**, designed to lead kids through the exhibits with thought-provoking questions and pictures. Imagine the scary voyage on board the over-crowded *Mayflower,* as "Saints" and "Strangers" crossed the Atlantic headed for lands unknown. Compare the ship models with paintings of the *Mayflower.* Experience the company's adventures and misfortunes for yourself!

Age Range: Kids 2-4 no; 5-10 yes, with Treasure Hunt Guide to keep on track; 10 and up yes.

Hours: Daily from 9:30 a.m. to 4:30 p.m.

Admission: Adults $5.00, seniors $4.00, kids (6-16) $2.50.

Time Allowance: 30 to 60 minutes.

Directions (55 miles from Boston): Take I-93 South to Rt. 3 South. Take Exit 4 and drive toward Plymouth. At the stoplight turn right on Main Street. (Rt. 3A). Pilgrim Hall will be 2 blocks down on the left.

Parking: Free; small lot behind museum.

Wheelchair Accessible: No.

Restaurant: No, but within easy walking distance.

Picnicking: No, but within easy walking distance.

Rest Rooms: Yes.

Gift Shop: Yes; books, glass trinkets, dolls, and candles.

KING RICHARD'S FAIRE
P.O. Box 419, Route 58
Carver, MA 02330
(508) 866-5391

FUN SCALE

If thou'dst like to step back in time to the 1600s, take a late summer's drive to Carver and spend the day at King Richard's Faire. The moment you leave your car, from the wooded area ahead the sounds of tambourines, lutes, singing gypsies, and applause permeate the air. Approach the castle-like facade and enter another time period: You're at a Renaissance fair in England; and everywhere you turn, you're surrounded by the 1600s.

I suggest you look at the schedule and plan your day's itinerary. There are scheduled events all day long and the shows overlap. You might begin by taking a stroll around the grounds.

If you're hungry or thirsty, your needs will easily be met. Almost everywhere you look there's a booth selling food or drinks from Roote Beere, to Chilly Bastard, to Castlemaine XXXX beers, and from Lamb on a Skewer or Roast'd Turkey Legge to mouthwatering desserts. Tickets can be purchased—and must be, if you want to eat—in $5.00 packs.

A word to the wise about money: You'll need to go armed with your pockets full of dollars. It's expensive. The initial entry fee includes all performances, but

ther costs range from pass-the-hat donations, to **Mystic Tarot** readings ($15.00), to attoos ($3.00 and up), to costume rentals ($10.00 to $35.00).

Entertainment abounds. In addition to the wandering minstrels, troubadours, stilt walkers, and costumed fairgoers, there are various scheduled performances, such as the **Mud Pit**, where you'll see mud beggars eat dirt for pay. There are gypsy dancers on the **Dance Stage** and puppets at the **Hellmouth Theater** and of course you don't

want to miss the "Royal Wedding" at the **King's Stage**. It begins with a wedding procession through the fairgrounds, after which a royal spoof of a wedding is performed gala style. The cast are well practiced and perform their comical roles animatedly. The other "don't miss" is "The Joust to the Death" over at the **Tournament Field**—action-packed battles between knights with lance and sword. The horses charge at full gallop as each knight tries to unseat his opponent. Upon contact, the fighters experience fifty-mile-per-hour impact. Splat!

Tests of strength, power, and skill abound. Muscled types will want to try the **Axe Throw** or **Giant Stryker**, while those who like games of skill may prefer the **Archer's Field** or **Dragon Joust**. For the younger folk, a ride on the **Swan Swing** or **Flying Carousel** will be sure to delight. Fun for all, and a nostalgic look back at entertainment before the days of MTV!

Age Range: Kids 2-4 no; 5-7 possibly, if not upset by the splattering blood packs in "The Joust to Death." The Dungeon exhibit (a comic history of medieval torture) should be avoided. Kids 8-10 are probably old enough to understand, though they might be uncomfortable with, some of the lewd humor of The Mud Show; but, will generally enjoy the Faire; kids 10 and up, yes.

Hours: From Labor Day Weekend Saturdays and Sundays until late October, from 11:00 a.m. to 6:00 p.m. Also open on Labor Day and Columbus Day.

Admission: Adults $14.00, children (5-10) $7.00.

Time Allowance: 2-4 hours.

Directions (55 miles from Boston): Take 93 South to 24 South to 495 South. Take Exit 2 (Rt. 58) and follow the signs.

Parking: Free and plentiful. A word to the wise: To avoid later hassles, make a mental note of some stationary object (not the car next to you) to remember your parking spot. Otherwise, the potential is there for frustration, big-time.

Wheelchair Accessible: Yes.

Restaurant: *Many* food stands.

Picnicking: Yes.

Rest Rooms: Yes.

Gift Shop: *Many* buyables scattered about in various booths.

A&D TOY AND TRAIN MUSEUM
49 Plymouth Street
Middleborough, MA 02346
(508) 947-5303

FUN SCALE

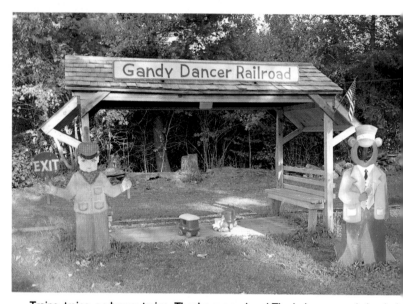

Trains, trains, and more trains. They're everywhere! The indoor space is loaded, and I mean jam-packed, with trains and toys. The majority are safely locked away behind glass, but there is *always* at least one electric train circling the room that is activated by you. Push the button and watch it travel through tunnels, across bridges, and around the artificial ponds. In addition to trains you'll find old-fashioned tin toys, foreign dolls, and science fiction memorabilia to look at.

When you've seen all there is to see indoors, step outside to the **Fun Park**. Have a picnic lunch, take a ride on the pedal train, play in the sand box, have a game of horseshoes, or climb aboard the mini-train and imagine yourself as the engineer. All aboard the Orient Express!

Age Range: Children 2-4 doubtful; 5 and up yes, if train buffs.
Hours: In July, August, and December, daily from 11:00 a.m. to 5:00 p.m. All other months Friday through Monday from 11:00 a.m. to 5:00 p.m.
Admission: Adults $5.00, seniors $4.50, kids (4-12) $3.50.
Time Allowance: About an hour.
Directions (42 miles from Boston): From I-495 South take Exit 6. Go left on Rt. 44 until you come to a rotary. Go three-quarters of the way around the rotary and head north on Rt. 18/28 for two miles. At the light, take a left. The museum is another three-quarters of a mile on your left.
Parking: Free and plentiful.
Wheelchair Accessible: Yes.
Restaurant: Coffee shop with hot and cold drinks, cookies, and doughnuts.
Picnicking: Yes.
Rest Rooms: Yes.
Gift Shop: Yes; train sets, model cars, cards, and engineer hats.

THE CHILDREN'S MUSEUM IN DARTMOUTH
276 Gulf Road
South Dartmouth, MA 02748
(508) 993-3361

FUN SCALE

If you've ever wondered where all of the kids are in Dartmouth when they're not at the beach, they're at the Children's Museum in Dartmouth. And with good reason. Its interactive exhibits promote creativity and inspire an interest in nature, science, and art. Explore two floors of fun in this big old converted dairy barn.

Start upstairs with the giant kinetic sculpture by Sig Purwin. Pushing the button twice activates the lights-a-flashing, funky road-building-equipment-styled piece of moving art. Then there's the **Medieval Room**, where you can try on some period clothes and act out a Middle Ages puppet show. There's more! Climb aboard the **Beetlecat Sailboat** and pretend to be in a gale

out at sea. Jump in the **Dune Buggy Car** and bounce along the sand dunes. Whip up a make-believe pizza meal after shopping in the **Supermarket Room**, equipped with mouth-watering rubber meats, veggies, canned goods, and a cash register. In the **Teddy Room** you'll find a cozy space with fireplace and piano to curl up and read a story.

Downstairs the fun continues. In the **Live Animal Room** you'll find turtles, bunnies, fish, ferrets, and parakeets. The **Construction Room** has pulleys, pumps, and architectural activities. Learn how to construct a Keystone Arch.

Outside is a new exhibit called **Windfarm**. What is energy? It's the ability to do work. At **Windfarm** you'll learn something about the principle of force times distance—as demonstrated by a windmill.

Age Range: Something for kids of any age.
Hours: Tuesday through Saturday from 10:00 a.m. to 5:00 p.m., Sunday from 1:00 to 5:00 p.m.
Admission: $3.75 per person (children under 1 admitted free). First Friday of every month, free from 5:00 to 8:00 p.m.
Time Allowance: 1 to 2 hours.
Directions (65 miles from Boston): Take I 195, to North Dartmouth (Exit 12 South). Proceed one mile, and turn left onto Rt. 6. At the first light, turn right onto Tucker Road. Go four miles, then turn left on Gulf Road. The museum is a quarter of a mile down the road on your right.
Parking: Free and plentiful.
Wheelchair Accessible: Windfarm and downstairs, yes. Upstairs, no.
Restaurant: No, but about a mile away.
Picnicking: Yes, tent outside.
Rest Rooms: Yes.
Gift Shop: Yes; yo-yos, kazoos, whistles, rubber snakes, and masks.

ZEITERION THEATER
684 Purchase Street
New Bedford, MA 02741
(508) 994-2900

FUN SCALE

Transport yourself to another place and time by taking in a performance at the Zeiterion Theater in New Bedford. There are scores of plays, puppet shows, dancing, and musical events for both kids and

adults. The performances happen in a red brick building done up in an ornate Georgian revival style and built in 1923. It's worth the trip.

Age Range: 4 and up, depending upon the show.
Hours: Show times vary.
Admission: Varies.
Time Allowance: Varies with show.
Directions (62 miles from Boston): From Rt. 195 take Exit 15 to Rt. 18 South. Continue to the first set of traffic lights and then take a right onto School Street. Go through three stop signs and turn right onto Purchase Street.
Parking: Meter and some free parking.
Wheelchair Accessible: Yes.
Restaurant: Small snack bar.
Picnicking: No.
Rest Rooms: Yes.

BUTTONWOOD PARK ZOO
PO Box C 804
New Bedford, MA 02741
(508) 991-6178

FUN SCALE

If you're in New Bedford and feel the urge to see some slow-moving wild animals in cages, you might go to the Buttonwood Park Zoo. The state-run zoo demonstrates the economic crunch at its fullest. It's the twelfth-oldest zoo in the USA, the third-oldest in New England, and the oldest zoo in continuous operation in Massachusetts.

As with all animals on the planet, they're impressive to look at. The day I was there, two Indian elephants were busy throwing hay on their backs—to protect them from sun and bugs, as I found out from the informational sign in the foreground. Did you know that an elephant can hold two gallons of water in its trunk and that it can drink sixty gallons of water a day? Read the sign.

Also in residence were a couple of owls, an American bison relaxing in a muddy cage, and a harbor seal playing dead man's float in its pool. At the periphery of the zoo were the deer and mountainous auodads from North Africa. It was impressive to drive along the street, look to the side and see the huge horned animals climbing on the boulders.

Don't expect to find a petting zoo. Funding doesn't allow the extra staff necessary for such an extravagance.

Although battling recession cutbacks, the park isn't lacking in space. Its ninety-six acres hold tennis courts, a baseball diamond, a playground, a pond, and a greenhouse. Check it out.

Age Range: For kids aged 2-4, there's nothing hands-on, so use your judgment; for 5 and up, a zoo is a zoo!
Hours: Daily from 10:00 a.m. to 4:00 p.m.
Admission: Adults $1.00, kids (under 12) 50¢.
Time Allowance: About an hour.
Directions (63 miles from Boston): From Interstate 195 take Exit 13A to 140 South; follow to the end. Turn left at the second set of lights, then take your first left and you're there.
Parking: Free and ample.
Wheelchair Accessible: Yes.
Restaurant: Daily pushcarts in summer; weekend pushcarts off-season.
Picnicking: Yes.
Rest Rooms: Yes.
Gift Shop: No.

NEW BEDFORD WHALING MUSEUM
18 Johnny Cake Hill
New Bedford, MA 02740
(508) 997-0046

FUN SCALE

New Bedford once played an important role in the whaling industry. For two hundred years the town's whaleships sailed the oceans seeking whalebone and oil for sale at home and abroad. The fascinating history of this period is preserved in New Bedford's one-of-a-kind Whaling Museum. Located on a hill with a view of the harbor, the museum and its extensive exhibits offer a unique chance to learn about the whaling industry—and have fun doing it.

Begin at the **Bourne Building** with the fifteen-minute orientation video. From the late eighteenth century and into the early twentieth, whale oil helped drive the economic growth of the country. Today, the museum contributes to the preservation of the whale through its educational programs and exhibits.

Also in the **Bourne Building** is the *Lagoda*, the world's largest model whaleship. At eighty-nine feet (and that's only a half-size model), the barkentine replica ship fills the room and is awesome, to say the least. Feel free to climb aboard! A hundred-foot whale mural by marine artist Richard Ellis serves as a backdrop to the *Lagoda*.

Exhibits include scrimshaw (whale bone art), paintings, glass objects, photographs, and eighteenth- and nineteenth-century toys. There's even a young humpback whale skeleton on the way into the theater, where you can sit and watch

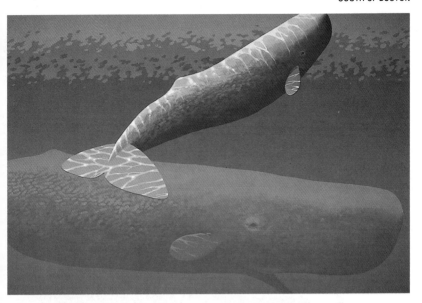

an eighteen-minute *National Geographic* video about humpbacks whales.

Age Range: Kids 2-4 might enjoy seeing the whale skeleton and playing at the *Lagoda's* helm; 5 and up yes, for varying amounts of time.

Hours: September through June, Monday to Saturday from 9:00 a.m. to 5:00 p.m., Sundays from 1:00 to 5:00 p.m. Also, Sundays in July and August from 11:00 a.m. to 5:00 p.m.

Admission: Adults $3.50, seniors $3.00, children (6-14) $2.50.

Time Allowance: 1-3 hours depending on the age.

Directions (62 miles from Boston): From Interstate 195 in New Bedford take Exit 15 and go one mile to Downtown Exit. Turn right on Elm Street, then left on Bethel Street. The museum is on the left in the second block.

Parking: Meters and garage.

Wheelchair Accessible: Partially.

Restaurant: No, but close by.

Picnicking: No.

Rest Rooms: Yes.

Gift Shop: Yes; books, sweat-and T-shirts, belaying pins, and fish hot pads.

BATTLESHIP MASSACHUSETTS
Battleship Cove
Fall River, MA 02721
(508) 678-1100

FUN SCALE

Battleship Cove is home to an extraordinary collection of old battleships for visitors to learn about and explore. You'll see firsthand how people fought at sea during World War II, and the Korean and Vietnam Wars.

Climb around on the battleship *Massachusetts* and walk the decks where sailors fought. Imagine manning the guns that defended the fleet during the Second World War. The nine decks provide you with a lot of exploration territory. See the galleys, mess halls, sleeping quarters, and one of the first computer rooms. Climb inside the turrets of the big guns and elevate the 40 mm anti-aircraft gun on the main deck. How does it feel to be defending the homeland at sea?

Duck your head and go inside the U.S.S. *Lionfish*, a W.W.II submarine that's still

perfectly intact. Imagine living, for weeks on end, in such cramped quarters. Not a space for claustrophics!

Board the destroyer, U.S.S. *Joseph P. Kennedy, Jr.,* named for the

oldest brother of President John F. Kennedy. It now houses the **National Destroyermen's Museum**. Push the button, look through the window, and listen to the fearful story of kamikazes, the Japanese pilots who flew planes loaded with bombs directly into ships back in 1944.

On your way out, check out the Japanese suicide demolition boat that was captured by the US fleet. It's a view of history you might not get anywhere else.

Age Range: Kids 2-4 no; 5-7 doubtful, unless the kid is a true battleship fan; 8-10 probably; 10 and up yes.
Hours: Daily from 9:00 a.m. to sunset.
Admission: Adults $8.00, kids (6-14) and seniors 4.00.
Time Allowance: 1-2 hours.
Directions (55 miles from Boston): Take Interstate 93 South to 128 South; take Rt. 24 South to Fall River and get off at Exit 7. Follow the small blue and white directional signs along the waterfront to Battleship Cove.
Parking: Free and plentiful.
Wheelchair Accessible: Limited access.
Restaurant: Snack bar.
Picnicking: Yes.
Rest Rooms: Yes.
Gift Shop: Yes; ship models, postcards, T-shirts.

THE FALL RIVER CAROUSEL
At Battleship Cove, P.O. Box 190
Fall River, MA 02722
(508) 324-4300

FUN SCALE

Whatever the weather you can still enjoy a ride on the magnificent horses and chariots of The Fall River Carousel. Enclosed in a modern, Victorian-style pavilion, the carousel overlooks **Battleship Cove** and such sights as the U.S.S. *Massachusetts* and the Fall River harbor. Prance to the music of an old-fashioned band organ! Carousels are exciting at any age, and this is a particularly fine one.

Age Range: Any age.
Hours: Memorial Day through Labor Day from 10:00 a.m. to 9:00 p.m. Call ahead for other times during the year.
Admission: 75¢ per ride, 10 rides for $6.00, Adult/child combo ride $1.00 (for children under 45 inches tall).
Time Allowance: 5 minutes.
Directions: See "Battleship Cove."
Parking: Free and plentiful.
Wheelchair Accessible: Yes.
Restaurant: Summer grill, winter snacks.
Picnicking: Yes, out in the park.
Rest Rooms: Yes.
Gift Shop: Yes.

MARINE MUSEUM AT FALL RIVER
70 Water Street
Fall River, MA 02721
(508) 674-3533

FUN SCALE

With battleships, sailboats, and yachts filling the harbor, what more appropriate place for a marine museum? This one is housed in an old mill building across from **Battleship Cove**. Inside you'll find a significant number of steamship models—over 150 of them, ranging in size from half an inch to twenty-eight feet. Notice the model of the *Charles E. Spahr*, a Japanese-built "baby super tanker" designed to transport four hundred thousand barrels of oil. Then there's the Fall River Line's *Puritan*, referred to as a "floating palace" because of its elegant interior and smartly dressed crew.

One of the most impressive pieces in the collection is the model of the *Titanic,* a one-ton, twenty-eight-foot replica of the famous, doomed ocean liner that sank on her maiden voyage in 1912 after hitting an iceberg. Kids will be especially interested to watch the seven-minute movie that goes with the exhibit and to hear the story of the *Titanic's* fatal crash in the frigid waters of the North Atlantic, in which hundreds of passengers were lost. This is a interesting stop on the Fall River tour, and very educational.

Age Range: Kids 2-4 no; 5-7 possibly, if ship enthusiasts; kids 8 years and up yes.
Hours: June to September, Monday through Friday, from 9:00 a.m. to 5:00 p.m. Weekends and holidays from 12:00 noon to 5:00 p.m. From October to May, Wednesday through Friday from 9:00 a.m. to 4:00 p.m. Weekends and holidays from 12:00 noon to 5:00 p.m.
Admission: Adults $3.00, Children $2.00.
Time Allowance: About an hour.
Directions: See "Battleship Cove."
Parking: Free.
Wheelchair Accessible: Yes.
Restaurant: No, but nearby.
Picnicking: No, but nearby.
Rest Rooms: Yes, across the street.
Gift Shop: Yes; patches, ship models, cards.

THE CHILDREN'S MUSEUM IN EASTON
The Old Fire Station, 9 Sullivan Avenue
North Easton, MA 02356
(508) 230-3789

FUN SCALE

Don't be fooled by the fire station facade. Inside is a real children's museum—a small-scale one compared with "the big one" in Boston, but definitely kid-friendly, with the added benefit of a more intimate, less overwhelming environment.

Play with the dinosaurs at the sand table. Step inside the simulated submarine and explore the deep. Climb the fire pole and see whether you can ring the bell. Paint your face and put on a play in the **Performance Center**. Admire the fish in the aquarium.

The themes and exhibits change regularly. There are also changing one-day workshops with topics on subjects such as "Math Marvels", "Food Fun", and "World of Motion."

Age Range: Kids 2-7 yes; 8 and up doubtful.
Hours: Tuesday through Saturday from 10:00 a.m. to 5:00 p.m., Sunday from noon to 5:00 p.m. Open some Monday holidays.
Admission: $3.50 per person. Under 2 free.
Time Allowance: 60 to 90 minutes.
Directions (30 miles from Boston): From Rt. 24 South take Exit 17B and follow Rt. 123 toward Easton. Then, again at the second light, turn right onto Rt. 138 North. At the second light, turn left on Main Street. Proceed for 1 mile and turn right on Sullivan Avenue.
Parking: Free.
Wheelchair Accessible: No.
Restaurant: No, but within walking distance.
Picnicking: Yes.
Rest Rooms: Yes, with infant safety seat.
Gift Shop: Yes; kazoos, bubble kits, tornadoes in a tube, volcano kits.

FULLER MUSEUM OF ART
455 Oak Street
Brockton, MA 02401
(508) 588-6000

FUN SCALE

Step into the world of art. The tranquil, woodsy setting provides the perfect backdrop for a somewhat unusual art museum. Opened in 1969, the wooden, multi-shingled modern building at the edge of a pond sets the stage for The Fuller Museum of Art.

Go up the ramp toward the door. The first piece of art is hard to ignore. You're surrounded by a whimsical creation of feathers and cables and bumpy pipes, all going every which way. Pull down the cord and listen. You've just rung a doorbell, of sorts.

Inside, there are (not literally) rotating exhibits, ranging from museum collection art to the work of featured artists. There are oodles of day-long workshops, as well as eight-week courses for kids. There's a program designed for children with special needs and another aimed at teaching the parent how to stimulate art appreciation in children. Innovative!

Age Range: 2-4 no, 5 and up yes, depending on exhibit or program.
Hours: Tuesday through Sunday from noon to 5:00 p.m., Thursdays until 9:00 p.m.
Admission: Donations accepted.
Time Allowance: 30 to 60 minutes.
Directions (18 miles from Boston): From Rt. 24 South take Exit 18B to Rt. 27 and bear right on Rt. 27 North. Take the first right onto Oak Street The museum is one mile ahead on your left.
Parking: Free.
Wheelchair Accessible: Yes.
Restaurant: Cafe open Tuesday through Friday from 11:00 a.m. to 2:00 p.m.
Picnicking: Yes, with permission.
Rest Rooms: Yes.
Gift Shop: Yes; artsy socks, jewelry, books, ceramics.

SOUTHWICK'S WILD ANIMAL FARM
Off Route. 16
Mendon, MA 01756
(508) 883-9182

FUN SCALE

Way out in the middle of Mendon's hills is one of the largest zoological collections in New England. If you don't believe me, go see for yourself! Southwick's Wild Animal Farm is the home of over a hundred species of animals, from exotic camels to common everyday sheep.

Roam around the three hundred acres and take in the wild sites. Having never before seen a kangaroo up close, I was impressed by its powerful tail and sharp claws. I learned a dromedary—a one-humped camel— can drink and store up to twenty-seven gallons of water at a time, and the unfortunate White Rhinoceros has a small brain and poor eyesight. Did you know its horn is made of compressed hair? My favorite animal there was the Vietnamese Pot-Bellied Pig. I never thought a pig could be cute, but these were.

Southwick's offers programs to increase individual awareness of the problems of animal endangerment. One of such programs, **Vanishing Animals**, is geared to high school age. Other programs include a wild animal orientation for grades K through 4, and one that addresses attitudes toward certain animals for grades 5 through 8.

In addition to the typical zoo scenes, there is a circus. Performed daily in the **Show Time Arena**, stars include an African elephant, llamas, and a crazy clown. Take a jaunt on a **Kiddieland Amusement** ride or cruise around on a real live elephant or pony. Groups can benefit from **Noah's Arkademy**, a building with live animal presentations, reptile exhibits, and educational displays.

ge Range: People of any age enjoy a zoo unless they're avid animal rights activists, but that's another ory.

ours: May through Labor Day, daily from 10:00 a.m. to 5:00 p.m. Limited hours in April, September, and ctober.

dmission: Adults $7.50, seniors $6.50, kids (3-12) $5.00.

me Allowance: 1-3 hours.

rections (40 miles from Boston): Take I 495 South to the Exit 20 and get on Rt. 16. Proceed toward endon turn left just past the center, and drive for about four miles. Look for the farm on your right.

arking: Free and plentiful.

heelchair Accessible: Yes.

estaurant: Yes, three snack stands.

cnicking: Yes.

est Rooms: Yes, with infant safety seat.

ift Shop: Yes; T-shirts, stuffed animals, puppets.

SOUTH OF BOSTON

MOTION ODYSSEY MOVIE RIDE
Jordan's Furniture
Avon, MA 02322
(508) 580-4900

FUN SCALE

It's an extraordinarily wild and, possibly, intensity-overload experience at the Motion Odyssey Movie (M.O.M.) Ride in Avon—an eighteen-minute spectacular collage of thrilling rides and excitement in your face.

Go in with an empty stomach; leave the Space Balls until after. Enter the preview room and experience a fascinating laser show as chest-thumping loud music and a smokey aroma permeate the air. The purpose is to ready you for what's to come. Follow the group to the next room. Strap yourself into the seat, place all belongings on the floor in front, sit back (forget about relaxing), hold on, and wait.

What you're about to experience is sensual stimulation—to the max. The computer-controlled seats tilt, bounce, jar, and swerve automatically with the action on the screen. In the opening scene you climb a skyscraper in an elevator, the door opens, and you walk right smack into the back of the person in front of you. That's nothing compared with what's about to come. After a falling scene from the very same skyscraper and landing on the roof of a police car (splat), you proceed to a dune buggy ride (bounce, bounce) in which you meet a tractor-trailer truck head-on (smash), race around hair-pin turns (screech), and finally end up in a high-speed chase through a narrow alley that looks like a futuristic scene from a science fiction movie. And then, of course there's the ongoing roller coaster ride. . .

Granted, there's not one iota of educational value involved, but it's wildly fun (for certain people) and all proceeds go to charity, which makes it even more worthwhile.

Age Range: The only M.O.M. age limitation is that the rider be a minimum of 40 inches tall so as to be able to hold the handles. Kids 2-4 no; 5-7 doubtful, but depends on TV-watching background and past acclimatizing/numbing experiences; 8 and up probably, if strong-stomached. (See M.O.M. Rules below).
Hours: Monday through Friday from 11:00 a.m. to 8:30 p.m., Saturday from 10:00 a.m. to 8:30 p.m., Sunday from 12:00 noon to 5:00 p.m.
Admission: Adults $4.00, (13 and under) $3.00.
Time Allowance: 18 minutes.
Directions (15 miles from Boston): From Rt. 24 South, take exit 19B.
At the lights take a right.
Parking: Free and plentiful.
Wheelchair Accessible: Yes, but it's a *long* trek through the store to get to M.O.M.
Restaurant: No; just snacks, soda, and Space Balls (freeze-dried ice cream).
Picnicking: No.
Rest Rooms: Yes.
Gift Shop: Yes; T-shirts, hats, boxer shorts—all with the M.O.M. logo.

M.O.M. Rules:
40 inches minimum height.
Good health.
Free from heart, back and neck problems, epilepsy, pregnancy, and motion sickness.
Young kids must be accompanied by adult.

THORNTON W. BURGESS MUSEUM
4 Water Street
East Sandwich, MA 02537
(508) 888-4668

FUN SCALE

Any Peter Rabbit fans out there? If you're going to be on the Cape, why not go to the museum of his possible creator? (It's uncertain whether Burgess or Beatrix Potter was the actual originator.) In this restored 1756 home, you'll find an extensive collection of Thornton Burgess's books, along with interactive displays and exhibits of his life and the natural history of Cape Cod. It's a small and intimate space where young children can explore the world of Peter Cottontail, Jimmy Skunk, and Grandfather Frog.

Push the button and listen to a five-minute story about the Visitors in Farmer Brown's Chicken Coop. Move into the **Dress-Up Room** and outfit yourself in a fox costume: head, tails, and paws. Stick your hands in the **Smiling Pools Mystery Box** and see whether you can identify the objects. "Eew gross, it's a mink pelt!" Create your own story, color it, and hang it on the wall of the museum. Hey, you can be famous!

During the summer, there are regularly scheduled story times with live animals that relate to the tales being told. Oh, and don't forget to pay a visit to the voracious swans and ducks in the pond before you leave—only resist the temptation to feed them: It's not allowed. It might be a good idea to combine this visit with a trip to **Heritage Plantation**.

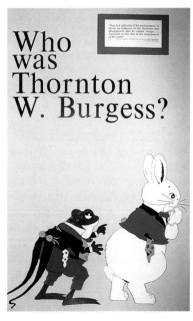

Age Range: Children 3-8 are the ideal age.
Hours: Monday through Saturday from 10:00 a.m. to 4:00 p.m., Sunday from 1:00 to 4:00 p.m. Winter hours vary.
Admission: Free, but donations are happily accepted.
Time Allowance: 30 minutes.
Directions (62 miles from Boston): Cross the Sagamore Bridge on Cape Cod. You're on Rt. 6 (Mid-Cape Highway). Get off at Exit 2 and go left on Rt. 130. Take a right on Water Street and you're there.
Parking: Free.
Wheelchair Accessible: Yes.
Restaurant: No.
Picnicking: Yes, next to the pond.
Rest Rooms: Yes.
Gift Shop: Yes; books, T-shirts, ceramic bunnies, Peter Rabbit book markers.

HERITAGE PLANTATION OF SANDWICH

Grove and Pine Streets
Sandwich, MA 02563
(508) 888-3300

FUN SCALE

The Heritage Plantation consists of seventy six acres of landscaped splendor dotted with a series of mini-museums devoted to objects of American antiquity. The gardens and grounds, constantly changing, are fun to visit at any time. The rhododendron bushes reach their peak in early June, for example, while the nine hundred-odd day lilies are at their height in early August, to name just a few of the plants

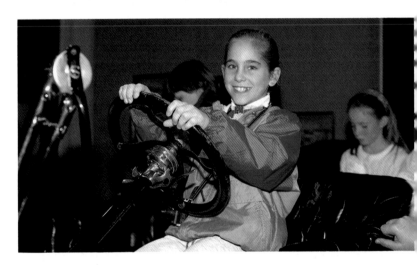

There's plenty to see in addition to the plants and flowers. The **Shaker Round Barn**, based on an authentic Shaker model, houses an impressive collection of antiqu and vintage cars. Automobiles weren't always powered by gasoline. Look for the little red car fueled by hot water. The Model-T Ford can be climbed on and is a favorite with school groups. Get behind the wheel and imagine yourself motoring along the roadways back in 1913. Cameras ready!

March over to the **Military Museum**, an unusual structure based on the Revolutionary period, where you'll find firearms and other military pieces from the Colonial period to the Spanish Civil War. Military buffs may enjoy the panoramas of battle scenes, with their scores of tiny soldiers; Kids may just like looking at the sword and guns. When was gunpowder invented? Visit the museum to find the answer. It also houses an extensive collection of Native American artifacts. By the way, the term "Indian" was first used by Christopher Columbus who thought he had landed in India. This misnomer has been used ever since. Today, Native American is a more accepte term.

Visit the **Old East Windmill**. Built in 1800, it could grind a bushel of grain, using wind power, in twenty minutes.

But the **Art Museum** may be the highlight of your day. First of all, there's a splendidly restored 1912 carousel that your kids are absolutely going to love. The nice part is that once you get your Heritage Plantation tickets, the carousel is free. The kids can have as many rides as they want—so be warned, you may be there a long time. The Upper Gallery of the museum contains collections of folk art. What's folk art? It's anything created by regular people with the purpose of being functional (usually) as well as nice to look at. The scrimshaw area is especially interesting.

The Lower Gallery contains a rotating collection of Currier and Ives lithographs. (Lithographs were big in the 1800s, before photography took over.)

For the less energetic, there's a shuttle bus that runs regularly around the grounds. It's free and stops at noted sites.

Age range: For kids 2-4, apart from the carousel, no; for those 5 and up, there's something to hold the interest of most, for varying degrees of time.

Hours: From Mother's Day in May until late October, daily from 10:00 a.m. to 5:00 p.m.

Admission: Adults $7.00, seniors $6.00, children(6-18) $3.50.

Time Allowance: 1-3 hours.

Directions (62 miles from Boston): Cross the Cape Cod

Sagamore Bridge and exit onto Rt. 6A. Take a right on Rt. 130 to Pine Street and Heritage Plantation.

Parking: Free and plentiful.

Wheelchair Accessible: Yes.

Restaurant: Yes, The Carousel Cafe.

Picnicking: Yes.

Rest Rooms: Yes.

Gift Shop: Yes; typical Americana tea towels, baskets, books.

NOAA FISHERIES AQUARIUM
Northeast Fisheries Science Center
166 Water Street, Woods Hole, MA 02543
(508) 548-7684

FUN SCALE

A chance to experience real, live animals up close can be thrilling. The Fisheries Aquarium in Woods Hole provides the opportunity for just that thrill, and everything is hands-on and close-up.

Before venturing inside, admire the seals frolicking in an outdoor pool during the summer months. If you're there during one of the two daily feeding times, 11:00 a.m. and 3:00 p.m., you'll get to watch a staff member playfully requesting tricks from the seals in return for tasty morsels of oceanic delicacies.

Inside there's a video about trash and its consequences. Did you know that

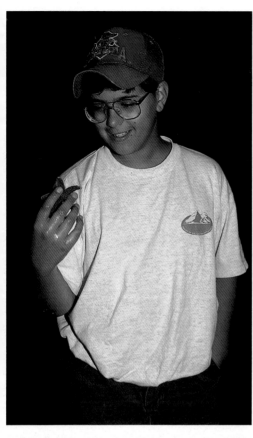

turtles die eating plastic and that those six-pack soda can rings kill? Animals get caught in them and die struggling to get out. Scenes like these serve as a reminder that the ecological balance is being threatened and we need to stop thoughtless littering to save it.

Next, check out the sixteen tanks of ocean creatures from the northeastern United States. There's an American lobster that weighs forty-two pounds. Startling! Look at the sharksuckers catching a ride on the backs of dogfish. They clamp down with their sucker-like discs and hang on for a free ride. Notice how those crazy dogfish swim. (They've learned to swim upright because, in the tanks, they're fed from above.)

Take a walk upstairs and get a glass-free view of the tanks—from above. Those gargantuan-looking fish are much smaller without the glass. Another popular attraction is the touch tank, low enough for kids to reach in and grab a slimy snail, squirmy crab, or a delicate whelk egg case.

Age Range: Any age will enjoy the aquarium.
Hours: Mid-June to mid-September, daily from 10:00 a.m. to 4:30 p.m. From mid-September to mid-June, Monday through Friday from 9:00 a.m. to 4:00 p.m.
Admission: Free.
Time Allowance: About an hour.
Directions (80 miles from Boston): Cross either of the Cape Cod bridges and take Rt. 28 toward Falmouth. Rather than turning left toward Falmouth center, bear right toward Woods Hole. Cross the drawbridge and continue straight until you reach the end of the road; turn right. The aquarium is on the left.
Parking: Meter and pay-lot.
Wheelchair Accessible: Yes.
Restaurant: No, but within walking distance.
Picnicking: No, but within walking distance.
Rest Rooms: Yes.
Gift Shop: No.

CAPE COD CHILDREN'S MUSEUM
Falmouth Mall, Rt. 28
East Falmouth, MA 02536
(508) 457-4667

FUN SCALE

In comparison with the enormous one in Boston, the Cape Cod Children's Museum may seem small in size, but it's bursting with fun, curiosity-stimulating experiences. Spark your desire to learn more.

Whisper into one whisper dish and have a partner stationed at the other dish. You'll hear each other clear across the room as if you were right next to each other. How does that work?

Create a meal in the make-believe diner set-up. Order something from a multicultural menu. Pretend to be a doctor in the mock ambulance and play with the stethoscopes and crutches, or read an x-ray. Climb aboard the thirty-foot pirate ship and sail out to sea.

In the **Bubble Room** you can make a gigantic bubble. In fact, you can completely surround yourself in a luminous film. Wave the magic bubble wand and presto! You're inside a bubble. Don't breathe!

Step into the **Space Station** and watch a movie about space exploration, with space tales from astronauts, parachutists, and other kinds of spacey people.

Fascinating!

The **Toddler Room**, designed for ages five and under, has stuffed animals, a dress-up room, and a veterinarian's area. Don't forget to splash around in the colored rice box. It's a favorite with the little guys.

Bigger kids love the **Shadow Room**. Pose, wait for the flash, and see your silhouette frozen on the wall. Look quickly, though; just as magically as it appeared, it will disappear.

Age Range: 2-10 yes; 10 and up doubtful.
Hours: Monday through Thursday and Saturday from 10:00 a.m. to 5:00 p.m., Friday from 10:00 a.m. to 8:00 p.m., Sunday from 12:00 noon to 5:00 p.m.
Admission: Ages 5-59 $3.00, 1-4 $2.00, 60 and up $2.00.
Time Allowance: 1 or 2 hours.
Directions (76 miles from Boston): After crossing the Bourne Bridge to Cape Cod, follow Rt. 28 toward Falmouth. Before coming to the center of town, take a left on Jones Road (the first intersection with a light) and proceed through two major intersections (1 mile). Look for signs for the Falmouth Mall on the left.
Parking: Free lot.
Wheelchair Accessible: Yes.
Restaurant: No, but within an easy walk.
Picnicking: No.
Rest Rooms: Yes, with a changing room.
Gift Shop: Yes; paint kits, dinosaur kits, sweat and T-shirts, rubber snakes and lizards.

CAPE COD SCENIC RAILROAD
252 Main Street
Hyannis, MA 02601
(508) 771-3788

FUN SCALE

For a bona-fide rail excursion, hop on the Cape Cod Scenic Railroad train in Hyannis and get a behind-the-scenes view of old Cape Cod. You and your kids will love riding the vintage trains, taking in the sights and listening to a commentary full of history, folklore, and information about the world passing by. Learn some cranberry facts while steaming past the bogs. Listen to tales of the forty thousand Wampanoag Indians back in the 1600s. There are 365 fresh-water ponds on Cape Cod. Look out at the world's widest sea-level canal, the seventeen-mile channel that divides the Cape from the mainland. Notice how the craft on the canal motor with or struggle against the strong current. In Sagamore, you'll turn around and make your way back to Hyannis.

If you wish, you may disembark in Sandwich and take a forty-minute

scenic bus tour, a trip to **Heritage Plantation**, or a combo trip to the **Sandwich Glass Museum** and the **Thornton Burgess Museum**. Later you may reboard at scheduled times and return to Hyannis.

Feel free to walk from car to car. Visit the snack bar, buy a pretzel, walk out back, and watch the tracks zip by below your feet. The magic of the rails!

Age Range: Kids 2-4 possibly; 5 and up yes.
Hours: From early June until late October, daily except Monday with four scheduled trips a day. Special Christmas trains on weekends from mid-November through mid-December.
Admission: Adults $10.50, seniors $9.50, kids (3-11) $6.50.
Time Allowance: 1 hour and 50 minutes.
Directions (80 miles from Boston): Once on Cape Cod, take Rt. 6 to Exit 6 to 132 South. From 132 South, at the airport rotary, take the Hyannis Center exit to Barnstable Road. Turn left on Center Street. When you hit the first set of lights, the station will be on the corner on your left.
Parking: Limited free lot and meter.
Wheelchair Accessible: No.
Restaurant: Yes, Cafe Car.
Picnicking: Yes.
Rest Rooms: Yes.
Gift Shop: Yes; T-shirts and caps.

THE CAPE COD MUSEUM
OF NATURAL HISTORY
Rt. 6A, Box 1710, Brewster, MA 02631
(508) 896-3867

FUN SCALE

Take a walk on the wild side with a visit to The Cape Cod Museum of Natural History. It's certainly smaller and more intimate than the sometimes-overwhelming Boston museums, but well worth a visit for young scientists at heart.

Start out by experiencing a mini-tornado. It's in a bottle, and you activate it by shaking it vigorously. Then stand back and let it rip!

Push a button and listen to the songs of the humpback whales while observing the museum's selection of gigantic whale bones. Don't miss the live hive loaded with honeybees. It's a hive of working bees connected to the great outdoors, and those bees are wild!

Elsewhere you'll find stuffed birds, from Eastern wild turkeys to Snowy owls, as well as tanks of fresh and salt-water fish—unlike the birds, very much alive! There's a space for puppet play-acting and other touchy things, like shell quizzes and magnifying-glass views of whelk egg case ribbons. No peeking when you try the **Touch and Guess Box**, full of hidden snails, fish skulls, and lobsters.

After a visit in the museum, take a walk on some of the eighty-two acres of trails or have a picnic lunch under the trees. A nice way to spend a day out.

Age Range: For 2-4s there are hands-on exhibits as well as story telling in the library; Kids 5 and up will enjoy the museum.
Hours: Monday through Saturday from 9:30 a.m. to 4:30 p.m., Sunday from 12:30-4:30 p.m.
Admission: Adults $3.50, children (6-14) $1.50.
Time Allowance: About 1 hour.
Directions (86 miles from Boston): Take the Mid-Cape Highway (Rt. 6) to Exit 9. Turn left on Rt. 134. Drive until Rt. 6A and turn left. The museum is about two miles ahead on the right.
Parking: Free and plentiful.
Wheelchair Accessible: Yes.
Restaurant: No.
Picnicking: Yes (uncovered).
Rest Rooms: Yes.
Gift Shop: Yes; stuffed animals, dinos, books, puzzles, musical rainsticks, tornado kits.

CAROUSEL VILLAGE
Roger Williams Park
Providence, RI 02905
(401) 785-9450

FUN SCALE

Carousel Village consists of a "chance" carousel and a mini-train ride. For those who are not carousel aficionados, a "chance" carousel is a newer plastic version of an older wooden carousel.

Age Range: Any age.
Hours: Early May to late October, daily from 11:00 a.m. to 5:30 p.m. Early November to late April, Friday from 10:30 a.m. to 4:00 p.m., Saturdays and Sundays from 11:00 a.m. to 5:00 p.m.
Admission: 75¢ per ride; 10 rides for $6.00.
Time Allowance: 4 minutes per ride.
Directions: See Roger Williams Park Zoo.
Parking: Free and ample.
Wheelchair Accessible: No.
Restaurant: No, but within walking distance.
Picnicking: Yes.
Rest Rooms: Yes.
Gift Shop: Yes, a few souvenirs.

ROGER WILLIAMS PARK ZOO
Elmwood Avenue
Providence, RI
(401) 785-3510

FUN SCALE

Located on 435 acres of Roger Williams Park, the zoo is the home of over 400 animals and birds. There's a lot to see, and you and the rest of the family can easily spend a full day taking in the sites.

As you walk through the zoo, you'll see the **Plains of Africa** with elephants, cheetahs, giraffes, and zebras. Speaking of zebras, do they have black or white stripes? Your background will determine the answer. People in America say black and people in Africa say white, generally. (By the way, there's no right or wrong answer.) Why does a big animal like a giraffe need a camouflaged coat? Because baby giraffes make tasty meals for lions and hyenas. Can the cheetah win the race against extinction? Questions like this, along with tidbits of interesting information, are offered by the African ranger props scattered about.

Look at the fabulous California sea lion as it dives in and out of the water. How can such a massive creature be so graceful in the water?

Check out the naked mole rats. These saggy little creatures look like

they're in someone else's body suit—besides needing the help of a good orthodontist!

The **Farmyard** is home to pigs, ducks, geese and even a bull. ¡Toro!

The Tropical America building is impressive. The hot, humid, smelly environment makes you feel as if you're ...ally there. Pick up a free guide to the exhibit and roam through: You'll see tree ...ngaroos, gila monsters, gigantic Colorado river toads, and bizarrely colored San ...ancisco garter snakes. Those Californians..!

Pretend you're a prairie dog. Climb under the prairie setup, and look up and ...rough the Plexiglas for a prairie dog's-eye view of life. Look out for the hawk!

...me Allowance: 30 to ...minutes, depending ...on number of houses ...sited.

...ours: April through ...ctober from 9:00 a.m. to ...00 p.m.; November ...rough March from 9:00 ...m. to 4:00 p.m.

...dmission: Adults ...50, kids (3-12), ...niors $1.50.

...me Allowance: 1 1/2 to ...hours.

...rections (49 miles from ...ston): From I 95 South ...ke Exit 17 (Elmwood ...enue). Turn left at the light and take your second left into the park.

...arking: Free and plentiful.

...heelchair Accessible: Yes.

...estaurant: Yes; Alice's Restaurant and the Hungry Bear Cafe.

...cnicking: Yes.

...st Rooms: Yes, with changing tables.

...ft Shop: Yes; blow-up dinosaurs, rubber snakes, animal shakers, cards.

155

THE CHILDREN'S MUSEUM
OF RHODE ISLAND
58 Walcott Street, Pawtucket, RI 02860
(401) 726-2591

FUN SCALE 🎈🎈🎈🎈

The Children's Museum of Rhode Island i located in the **Pitcher-Go** **Mansion**, an 1840 architectural treasure in th historic district of Pawtucket. Step inside an explore for yourselves.

There's plenty there to capture your attention. You might begin by whipping up an imaginary meal in **Great-Grandmother's Kitchen**. In this original nineteenth-century mansion kitchen, you and the kids can create a plaster fruit pie and set it to bake in the cast-iron stove. While you're waiting for it to brown, you might scrub a few clothes in that gigantic old wash tub, or mend your soc with the foot-pedal sewing machine. Ah, the good old days!

Pick up a few tips about architecture in **Our House**. A playhouse-sized model c the museum provides the setting for architectural exploration and for learning about t various tools and building parts. Put on a hard hat, pick up a hammer, and go to town

In **My Way Your Way**, you can learn about what life is like for someone who's blind, confined to a wheelchair, or dyslexic. Gain an understanding of disabilities as you experiment with wheelchairs, menus in braille, and other tools; nearby videos demonstrate a few of the many possibilities for disabled persons. The exhibit can be a real eye-opener.

Climb the stairs and say hello to the oversized stuffed figure named **Estrella** at the top. Believe me, you can't miss her! Feel free to

imb into her
mense lap;
e's perfectly
endly. A word
f warning for
arents with
ounger
ildren,
ough: She
oesn't mean
, but she
cares the heck
ut of some of
e kids. Use
our judgment.

In the **Shape Lab**, visitors can explore geometric shapes amid huge, brightly
colored tetrahedrons, octahedrons, and dangling cubes. A member of your family
ight just be inspired to create his or her own geometric shapes. Is it math or is it art?

ge Range: Kids 2-7 yes; 8-10 possibly; 10 and up doubtful.

Hours: Tuesday
through Saturday from
9:30 a.m. to 5:00 p.m.,
Sunday from 1:00 to
5:00 p.m.
Admission: $3.50 per
person.
Time Allowance: 1 to 2
hours.
Directions (45 miles
from Boston): From I-95
South heading toward
Pawtucket, take Exit 29
(Downtown Pawtucket).
Keep right on Broadway
for a quarter mile, pass
the Exchange Street

ht, and turn left into the museum parking lot.
rking: Free off-street parking.
heelchair Accessible: Yes, first floor only.
staurant: No, but within easy walking distance.
cnicking: No.
st Rooms: Yes, with infant safety seats.
ft Shop: Yes; stuffed dinosaurs, yo-yos, ants, pins, and books.

Rhode Island

MUSEUM OF NATURAL HISTORY
Roger Williams Park
Providence, RI 02905
(401) 785-9450

FUN SCALE

Visitors can discover the present as well as the distant past through the natural history of this planet. Look at the geology displays of rocks from zillions of years ago. How did they get here? Other exhibits include an impressive insect display—fascinating, if you're into some pretty scary-looking bugs—and one that captures the wonders of polar bears in their Arctic environment.

Learn about the excitement of space exploration and explore the moon yourself through a powerful telescope—yes, you can see it during the day. Can you fathom the idea of actually rocketing to the moon? To investigate the mysteries of outer space even further, reach for the stars and catch a Planetarium show. Well worth a visit if you're in the area.

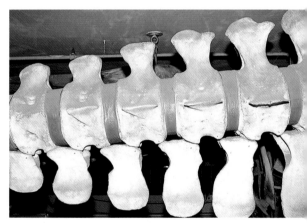

Age Range: Kids 2-4 no; 5-7 possibly, but not much is hands-on; 8 and up yes.
Hours: November to March, Tuesday through Friday from 10:00 a.m. to 4:00 p.m.; Saturday and Sunday from 11:00 a.m. to 4:00 p.m. April to October, Tuesday through Friday from 10:00 a.m. to 4:00 p.m.; Saturday and Sunday from noon to 5:00 p.m. Closed Mondays except Monday holidays.
Admission: Free. The Planetarium costs $1.00 for adults and 50¢ for kids over age 4. (Under age 4 not admitted.)
Time Allowance: About an hour.
Directions: See Roger Williams Park Zoo.
Parking: Free and ample.
Wheelchair Accessible: No, but under construction.
Restaurant: No, but within walking distance.
Picnicking: Yes.
Rest Rooms: Yes.
Gift Shop: Yes, small.

Rhode Island

HAMMERSMITH FARM
Ocean Drive
Newport, RI 02840
(401) 846-0420

FUN SCALE

For a taste of Newport opulence, go visit Hammersmith Farm. Guided tours run regularly through this twenty-eight room, shingle-style summer "cottage" overlooking Narragansett Bay. The number of bathrooms alone is astonishing; there are seventeen! Hammersmith Farm was the summer house of Jacqueline Bouvier, and the site of her marriage to John F. Kennedy. During the years of 1961-1963, it became known as the Newport "Summer White House." It's loaded with history, and the house tour provides a knowledgeable guide to answer all questions. It's a hands-off, no-photo situation, but well worth the tour.

Following the house tour, stroll out through the grandiose gardens designed by Frederick Law Olmstead, the landscape architect of Central Park in New York City. Passing among the meticulously manicured lawns, meander out to the "farm" area. Jackie was very fond of her miniature horses. You're not allowed to touch or feed them, but the tiny horses are adorable and lots of fun to look at. And don't forget to admire the goats, miniature donkey, guinea hens, and peacocks.

Age Range: Kids 2-7, definitely not: The house and the gardens are "Do not touch," making it difficult for little squirmers. Kids 8-10 will appreciate the gardens and possibly the "cottage"; Kids 10 and up, yes.
Hours: From the 3rd weekend in March to mid-November, daily from 10:00 a.m. to 5:00 p.m.
Admission: Adults $6.50, children (6 and under) $3.00.
Time Allowance: About an hour.
Directions (72 miles from Boston): Once in Newport, follow the signs for Ocean Drive and Fort Adams State Park; Hammersmith Farm is just beyond the park.
Parking: Free.
Wheelchair Accessible: Outside space only.
Restaurant: No.
Picnicking: No.
Rest Rooms: Yes.
Gift Shop: Yes; located in what was the children's playhouse—cookbooks, JFK stationary, plants.

THE RHODE ISLAND FISHERMAN AND WHALE MUSEUM
18 Market Square, Newport, RI 02840
(401) 849-1340

FUN SCALE

Most of Newport may be "hands-off" or "keep-off," but not The Rhode Island Fisherman and Whaling Museum. *Au contraire*, it's almost all hands-on, with an educational, fun approach.

Have you ever been curious about knot tying, feeling some whale blubber, listening to real-live fishermen on a marine radio, looking at a lobster's anatomy, or harvesting a few quahogs? Now's your chance in this interactive museum.

Look through a microscope and learn what's in a drop of plain old sea water. You'll definitely close your mouth the next time you go swimming!

In the **Whale Room** you'll see giant whale bones. See whether you can match the whales' tails. Compare a dolphin skeleton with a human skeleton and try to match the bones. What's it like to be covered in whale blubber? Put your hands in the blubber box.

Look at the three aquariums in the **Narragansett Bay Room**. Can you find the eighteen-inch fish hiding in the sand? Test your skill at matching the fish with the

names next to the push buttons.

In the **Fishing Room**, try on some foul-weather gear and climb into the wheelhouse, which is fully equipped with a Loran, helm, and throttles. Check out the lobster anatomy model. Pick up the huge tongs and test your skills at quahogging. What the heck *is* a quahog anyway? Does anyone know?

Age Range: For kids 2-4 there are a lot of hands-on activities; older kids will enjoy most of the displays.
Hours: Open every day except Wednesday from 10:00 a.m. to 5:00 p.m.
Admission: Adults (13 and up) $2.50, children (2-12) $1.50.
Time Allowance: 30-90 minutes.
Directions (72 miles from Boston): Go to the center of Newport and find the harbor. Just off of Thames Street is Bowen's Wharf. The museum is in the Seamen's Church Institute on the second floor.
Parking: Meters along Thames Street, pay-lots scattered about, and free public two-hour parking (watch the chalk-marking meter maids).
Wheelchair Accessible: No.
Restaurant: No, but millions nearby.
Picnicking: No.
Rest Rooms: Yes.
Gift Shop: Small, but good-quality rubber animals, fish stickers, wooden killer whale models.

AQUIDNECK LOBSTER
Bowen's Wharf
Newport, RI 02840
(401) 846-0106

FUN SCALE

After visiting **The Rhode Island Whale and Fishing Museum**, hold your nose and walk over to Aquidneck Lobster. Take a stroll past the lobster tanks; if you're lucky you'll catch a glimpse of a fishing boat unloading the catch of the day. Look at all those claws! The bigger the lobster, the older it is. Ask to see the blue lobster. Strike up a conversation with one of the employees: They're animated and friendly.

Hours: Daily from 6:30 a.m. to 7:30 p.m.
Admission: Free.
Directions (72 miles from Boston): Just off of Thames Street is Bowen's Wharf. At the end of the wharf is Aquidneck Lobster.
Parking: Meters along Thames Street, pay-lots scattered about, and occasional free 2-hour public parking.
Wheelchair Accessible: No.

THE INTERNATIONAL TENNIS HALL OF FAME
194 Bellvue Avenue, Newport, RI 02840
(401) 849-3990

FUN SCALE

Housed in the Newport Casino—not to be confused with a gambling hall—The International Tennis Hall of Fame contains the world's largest collection of tennis memorabilia. The hall (casino means "little house" in Italian) is dedicated to the preservation, history, and heritage of tennis.

Although it's a minimally hands-on situation, the exhibits will be of interest to young tennis buffs. It's a self-guided tour through rooms and rooms of tennis memorabilia. See the racket that Chris Evert used to win the 1982 US Open next to the sneakers that led her to victory in the 1983 French Open. Notice the dinosaur version of Jimmy Connors' Wilson T-2000, the racket with which he won the US Open in 1983. Visit the Women in Tennis room. Challenge yourself with the video question "touch" games and test your knowledge of tennis trivia.

Take a walk outside and see the thirteen grass courts that host both amateur and professional tournaments; along with a clay court, they are available for public use.

Age Range: Kids 2-4 no; 5-7 probably not; 8 and up yes, if avid tennis fans.
Hours: Daily from 10:00 a.m. to 5:00 p.m.
Admission: Adults $6.00, Children under 16 $3.00, Family $12.00.
Time Allowance: 30-60 minutes.
Directions (72 miles from Boston): 1 block away from and parallel to the harbor is Bellvue Ave.
Parking: Meter or free lot across the street.
Wheelchair Accessible: No.
Restaurant: No, but close by.
Picnicking: No.
Rest Rooms: Yes.
Gift Shop: Yes; tennis clothes, bags, cards, books, magnets.

GREEN ANIMALS TOPIARY GARDENS
Narragansett Bay
Portsmouth, RI 02840
(401) 683-1267

FUN SCALE

The Alice Brayton House, built in 1872, is a well-preserved Victorian summer residence overlooking the Narragansett Bay. It also houses the toy museum, containing nineteenth-century dolls, soldiers, books, and other assorted toys. It's a "no-touch" situation, so young kids might be bored.

Outside, take a stroll through the freshly raked paths and carefully manicured grounds of the gardens. **The Upper Topiary Lawn** consists of privet and yew bushes trained to resemble animals and geometric shapes. Teddy Bear and Spot the Dog are two of the favorites. Don't forget to look for goldfish in the fish pond.

Age Range: Kids 2-4 no, nothing is hands-on; 5-7 will enjoy seeing the topiary garden; 8 and up will appreciate the toy museum and topiary garden.
Hours: May 1 to October 31, daily from 10:00 a.m. to 5:00 p.m.
Admission: Adults $6.00, children (6-11) $3.00.
Time Allowance: About an hour.
Directions (62 miles from Boston): Take Rt. 24 South to Rt. 114 South. Drive 3/10 mile and turn right on Cory's Lane. Follow to end.
Parking: Free.
Wheelchair Accessible: Yes, on the grounds and first floor of the house.

Restaurant: No, only a soda machine.
Picnicking: Yes, on lawn in front of house.
Rest Rooms: Yes.
Gift Shop: Yes; books, toys, juggling kits, fish pencil cases.

FESTIVALS AND OTHER NOTEWORTHY EVENTS

JANUARY
Chinese New Year

Look for the giant dragon dancing through the streets and listen for the firecrackers. The dragon scares the devil away and leads the good luck in. It all happens at Beach and Tyler Streets in Boston on a Sunday afternoon.

FEBRUARY
Black History Month

There are a variety of events designed especially for kids hosted by area museums and libraries.

MARCH
Saint Patrick's Day Parade

Boston has a large and active Irish community. St. Patrick's Day is a festive event.

APRIL
Big Apple Circus

An intimate approach to a circus. It's small enough for a close-up view, and big enough to fascinate the viewers. The circus people actually seem to care about the animals. Call the Children's Museum for information. (617) 426-6500.

The Boston Marathon

A twenty-six mile race from Hopkington to the Prudential Center; one of the most popular marathons in the country.

MAY
Kite Festival

On the second or third Saturday in May, Franklin Park in Dorchester hosts a kite event including kite flying, kite making clinics, and kite contests. Call (617) 635-4505

JUNE
Boston Common Dairy Festival

As in the olden days, you'll see cows, ducks, chickens, and sheep grazing on the Common while you eat ice cream galore (not as in the olden days). Call (617) 635-4505.

Teddy Bear Picnic

Bring your picnic and teddy bear for a night on the town on Boston Common. Sample the entertainment and foods. Check out the other teddies too! (617) 635-4505.

JULY
Puerto Rican Festival

Five days of the best salsa music, folklore and storytelling, crafts, and *El Dia de los Ninos:* a full day of amusement rides, carnival games, clowns, a parade, and heaps of ethnic foods. *¡Que rico!* Call (617) 635-4505

165

AUGUST
Caribbean-American Festival
A week-long, popular, and colorful celebration beginning with a Children's Carnival. Thousands of revelers dance through the streets to the music of calypso, steel bands, and reggae. Call (617) 534-5832.

Chinese Moon Festival
It takes place during the August full moon in Chinatown. The streets are blocked off to allow a parade, martial arts demos, and song and dance.

Festival of Hope
A celebration on Boston Common using school programs to promote peace. All done to the tune of music, food, and live entertainment. Call (617) 635-4920.

SEPTEMBER
Leaf peeking and cranberry-harvest viewing galore! Take a ride in the country.

OCTOBER
Massachusetts Cranberry Harvest Festival
The festival celebrates the harvest season through demonstrations and good food. Located in South Carver and free to the public.

NOVEMBER
Winter Wonderland
This runs from late November until late December on Boston Common. Experience train and merry-go-round rides, tree decorating, and snow persons (weather permitting). Call (617) 635-4505.

DECEMBER
First Night
New Year's Eve in Boston. All kinds of entertainment for every age: ice sculptures, mime, BMX bike demonstrations, reggae music, and folk dancing, to name a few. Some are free, most are not. Call (617) 542-1399.

GREAT BEACHES

CRANE BEACH RESERVATION
290 Argilla Road, Ipswich, MA 01938
(508) 356-4351
Other than during the nasty black fly season (check first, it changes), Crane Beach offers a peaceful, pleasant experience. There are tide pools for shell exploration, spacious beaches, and miles of nature trails.

Directions (37 miles from Boston): Take 128 North to exit 20A. Get on Rt. 1A North for 8 miles. Turn right on Rt. 133 East and continue for 1 1/2 miles before turning left on Northgate Road. At the end turn right on Argilla

166

Road. Go to the end.
Parking: Summer season $12.00 per car on weekends and holidays, $8.00 per car on weekdays. Half price on Mondays and Tuesdays. Off-season $4.00 per car on weekends, $3.00 per car on weekdays.
Restaurant: Snack bar.
Rest rooms: Yes, with showers.

DUXBURY BEACH PARK
Duxbury, MA 02331

A spacious wide-open beach with white sand and aqua-blue water. Walk along the endless stretch of sand and take an occasional dip. What could be more enticing? Sometimes, on busy summer weekends, the parking lot fills. Arrive early.

Directions (50 miles from Boston): Take I 93 South to Rt. 3 South to Exit 11. Take Rt. 14 East to Rt. 139 West and go two miles. At Canal Street, turn and bear right until you're on Gurnet Road. The beach is straight ahead at the end of the road.
Parking: $8.00 on weekend days, $5.00 on weekdays in the summer (1 week before Memorial Day until two weeks after Labor Day).
Restaurant: Snack bar.
Rest rooms: Yes, with showers. 50¢ per shower.

FALMOUTH HEIGHTS BEACH
Grand Avenue, Falmouth, MA 02540
(508) 548-8623

Spacious, but potentially crowded in the summer. It's supposed to be a "residential" beach, but if you can find parking, you can use the beach. Watch the parking meter.

Directions (78 miles from Boston): Follow Rt. 28 through the center of Falmouth and when the road curves around to the left, turn right on Falmouth Heights Road. At the end, bear left on Grand Avenue.
Parking: Meter only.
Restaurant: Yes.
Rest Rooms: No.

GOOD HARBOR BEACH
Gloucester, MA 01930
(508) 283-1601

A wonderfully kid-friendly beach. There's a close tidal pool for digging and exploring the ocean's creatures, and further out is the deep blue sea.

Directions (38 miles from Boston): Take 128 North to the very end and turn left. The beach is about three miles beyond Gloucester Center.
Parking: $15.00 per day during the summer season.
Restaurant: Yes, snack bar.
Rest Rooms: Yes, with showers.

HORSENECK BEACH
P.O. Box 328, Westport Point, MA 02791
(508) 636-1000

A long, wide sandy beach opening on to Rhode Island Sound, and backed by high, beautiful sand dunes, this state-run beach is one of the finest in Southern New

England. There are no tidepools for kids to explore, but the surf is usually mild-just right for kids.

Directions (70 miles from Boston): Take Rt. 195 to Rt. 88, and follow ten miles to the beach.
Parking: $2.00 per car from May 27 through Labor Day.
Restaurant: Yes, snackbar.
Rest Rooms: Yes, with showers.

NANTASKET BEACH
Nantasket Avenue, Hull, MA 02045
(617) 925-1777

A three-mile stretch of sand along the wide-open Atlantic Ocean. Although it may seem to be dangerously close to Boston harbor, it's far away enough to avoid the harbor backwash, and to be a clean and pleasant beach.

Directions (15 miles from Boston): Take I-93 South to Rt. 3 South. Get off at Exit 14 and follow Rt. 228 to Nantasket.
Parking: Pay-lot during the summer.
Restaurant: Yes.
Rest Rooms: Yes.

OLD SILVER BEACH
Quaker Road, North Falmouth, MA 02556
(508) 548-8623

A small and sometimes very crowded, but popular beach. As one teenager put it, "That's where the fine guys go."

Directions (76 miles from Boston): Follow Rt. 28 to the Exit for Rt. 151 and North Falmouth. Turn left off of the exit and then left again on Rt. 28A. Follow for about two miles and turn right on Quaker Road. Continue about one mile until you see the beach on the right.
Parking: $5.00 per day during the summer season.
Restaurant: Snack bar.
Rest Rooms: Yes, with showers.

PAINE'S CREEK BEACH
Paine's Creek Road, Brewster, MA 02631

A "best of" for kid-friendly beaches. Depending on the status of the tide, it's usually loaded with shells and turn-overable rocks for beach exploration. Paine's Creek Beach is one of seven continuous beaches that line the shores of Brewster.

It's possible to walk through the trails from The Cape Cod Museum of Natural History to the beach. Why not spend a day natural historying in the morning and beaching in the afternoon? Perfect!

Directions (86 miles from Boston): Cross the Sagamore Bridge on Cape Cod and you're on Rt. 6. Take Exit 10 and follow Rt. 124 to Rt. 6A. Take a left on Rt. 6A and drive until you see Luke's Liquors on the right. Turn down Paine's Creek Road and continue to the end.
Parking: $8.00 per day for non-residents.
Restaurant: Mobile hot dog wagon.
Picnicking: Yes.
Rest Rooms: Yes.

SINGING BEACH
Manchester, MA 01944
(508) 526-1731

Singing Beach is named for the sound the sand makes under your toes when you walk on it. Take your shoes off, shuffle along, and listen! The beach is wide open and sandy, and on the right there is a mini-tide pool to dig around in.

Directions (36 miles from Boston): Take the commuter train to Manchester and walk about half a mile to the beach.
Parking: Unless you're one of the few lucky people to get a space in the beach lot during the week, you will park half-a-mile away in a lot in town. The cost is $15.00 per day. The admission fee for the beach on Friday through Monday is $1.00.
Restaurant: Snack bar.
Rest Rooms: Yes, with cold showers.

STAGE FORT PARK BEACHES
Gloucester, MA 01930
(508) 283-1601

The two beaches at Stage Fort Park are Half Moon Beach and Cressey Beach. Half Moon Beach is cool because, to get there, you need to climb up the rock-carved steps and down into the secret beach below. The Cressey Beach is larger, more open, and has more rocks. They both look out at Gloucester harbor.

Directions (39 miles from Boston): Take 128 North to Exit 14. Turn right on Rt. 133 heading toward Gloucester and turn right at the end. The park is approximately a quarter of a mile ahead on the left.
Parking: $15.00 per day during the summer season.
Restaurant: Yes.
Rest Rooms: Yes, but no showers.

SURF DRIVE
Surf Drive, Falmouth, MA 02540
(508) 548-8623

A long, narrow town beach looking out at Martha's Vineyard. There's a small wading area. As with most public beaches, it gets crowded in the summer.

Directions (76 miles from Boston): Follow Rt. 28 into the center of Falmouth. Just past the library green, take a right on Surf Drive. Follow it to the end and you're there.
Parking: $5.00 per day during the summer season.
Restaurant: Snack bar.
Rest Rooms: Yes, with a shower.

WINEAGERSHEEK BEACH
West Gloucester, MA 01930
(508) 283-1601

Wineagersheek (pronounced "Wingersheek") has zillions of rocks and shells to turn over and investigate, and a football-field sized sandbar during low tide.

Directions (38 miles from Boston): Take 128 North to Exit 13. Turn left and it's about three miles ahead.
Parking: $15.00 per day during the summer season.
Restaurant: Yes, snack bar.
Rest Rooms: Yes, with showers.

CLOSEST CROSS-COUNTRY SKI PLACES

WESTON SKI TRACK
Park Road, Weston, MA 02193
(617) 891-6575

Weston Ski Track offers a chance to ski or learn to ski, and it's exceptionally close to Boston. It's fully equipped with snowmaking machines for those non-snowy winters, as well as lights for night skiing. Rentals, sales, and instructions available.

Directions (8 miles from Boston): Take the Massachusetts Turnpike (I 90) West to Exit 15. Bear to the left toward Rt. 30, and at the end of the exit, turn left on Park Road. Weston Ski Track is ahead on the left.
Restaurant: Yes; snack bar
Rest Rooms: Yes.

GREAT BROOK STATE FARM
841 Lowell Street, Carlisle, MA 01741
(508) 369-6312

Ninety acres of trails over the farmland. A hut with a fireplace provides warmth, hot food and drinks, and equipment rentals.

Directions (22 miles from Boston): Take Rt. 128 North to Rt. 225 West to Carlisle Center. Turn right on Lowell Street. The farm is two miles ahead on the right.
Restaurant: No, but snack bar.
Rest Rooms: Yes.

WACHUSETT MOUNTAIN
499 Mountain Road, Princeton, MA 01540
(508) 464-2300

Eleven and a half miles of trails originating near the lodge. Limited lessons and rental equipment available; call first.

Directions (55 miles from Boston): Take Rt. 2 West to Exit 25 and go onto Rt. 140 South.
Restaurant: Yes.
Rest Rooms: Yes.

PONKAPOAG GOLF COURSE
2167 Washington Street, Canton, MA 02021
(617) 828-5828

This gigantic golf course turns into a good cross-country ski space in the winter; in fact, it has the reputation of being the best around. Respite from the cold and a cup of hot chocolate are provided at the Metropolis Ice Rink next door. No snow making or trail grooming. Free.

Directions (15 miles from Boston): Take I 93 South to Exit 2A (Canton). Turn left at the end of the exit. The course is less than a mile down Rt. 138 South.
Restaurant: No, but there's a snack bar in the Metropolis Ice Rink.
Rest Rooms: No, but facilities available in the Metropolis Ice Rink.

CLOSEST DOWNHILL SKI PLACES
BLUE HILLS SKI AREA
4001 Washington Street, Milton, MA 02186
(617) 828-5090

Incredibly close to Boston with terrain for beginners to experts. Seven slopes with a chair lift, two J-bars, and a pony lift. Blue Hills has snow-making equipment and equipment rentals.

Directions (5 miles from Boston): Take I 93 South to Exit 2B (Rt. 138 North). The ski area is one-half a mile down on the right, next to the Trailside Museum.
Restaurant: Yes.
Rest Rooms: Yes.

WACHUSETT MOUNTAIN
499 Mountain Road, Princeton, MA 01540
(508) 464-2300

This kid-friendly ski center offers "Skiwee" classes for ages three to twelve, with a special Polar Playground of roller coaster bumps, bobsled runs, and hula hoops where kids can have fun while learning the basics and before riding the sometimes-scary lifts. Polar Cub Den is an indoor space for "Skiwee" kids to warm up and have a bite to eat. Polar Cub Nursery is a baby-sitting service for kids aged three months to four years. Reservations are necessary for the Nursery. Lifts include three chair lifts, one pony and one poma lift. The lodge has four eating areas, snowmaking equipment, and ski rentals.

Directions (55 miles from Boston): Take Rt. 2 West to Exit 25 and to Rt. 140 South.
Restaurant: Yes.
Rest Rooms: Yes.

INDEX